Social Studies

Grade 4

Photo credits: 3 ©Ryan McVay/Photodisc/Getty Images; 5 ©Corbis Royalty Free; 7 ©FPG International/Getty Images; 13 ©Library of Congress; 14 ©Jupiterimages/Polka Dot/Alamy; 17 ©image100/Age Fotostock America, Inc.; 18 ©Getty Images/Digital Vision; 26 (tl) ©Getty Images/PhotoDisc; 26 (tr) ©Getty Images/Photodisc; 28 ©Comstock/Getty Images; 33 ©Scenics of America/PhotoLink/Photodisc/Getty Images; 34 (t) ©C. Borland/PhotoLink; 34 (b) ©Photodisc/Getty Images; 42 (t) ©Getty Images; 42 (b) ©Getty Images/PhotoDisc; 46 © Ocean/Corbis; 47 ©Scenics of America/PhotoLink/Getty Images; 48 ©Digital Vision/Getty Images; 58 ©Corbis; 60 ©Hemera Technologies/Getty Images; 63 ©Radius Images/Alamy Images; 64 ©Kim Steele/Photodisc/Getty Images; 65 ©Digital Vision/Getty Images; 66 ©Photodisc/Getty Images; 73 (t) ©Digital Vision/Getty Images; 73 (b) ©forcdan/Fotolia; 77 ©Joseph Sohm-Visions of America/Photodisc/Getty Images; 78 ©Photodisc/Getty Images; 79 ©Photodisc/Getty Images; 80 ©PhotoDisc/Getty Images Royalty Free; 81 (l) ©Photodisc/Getty Images; 81 (r) ©Digital Vision/Getty Images; 87 ©Corbis; 92 © Scenics of America/PhotoLink/PhotoDisc/Getty Images; 93 ©Photodisc/Getty ©Images; 97 ©Corbis; 103 ©W9 2000 INC/Photodisc Green/Getty Images; 105 ©Charles Douglas Peebles/Alamy; 109 ©Hemera Technologies/Getty Images; 111 R. Morley/PhotoLink/Getty Images; 112 ©Digital Vision/Getty Images; 113 (l) ©Getty Images/Photodisc; 113 (r) ©J. Luke/Getty Images; 114 ©Getty Images Royalty Free/Eyewire; 115 ©Corbis

Copyright © 2014 by Houghton Mifflin Harcourt Publishing Company

All rights reserved. No part of this work may be reproduced or transmitted in any form or by any means, electronic or mechanical, including photocopying or recording, or by any information storage or retrieval system, without the prior written permission of the copyright owner unless such copying is expressly permitted by federal copyright law.

Permission is hereby granted to individuals to photocopy entire pages from this publication in classroom quantities for instructional use and not for resale. Requests for information on other matters regarding duplication of this work should be addressed to Houghton Mifflin Harcourt Publishing Company, Attn: Contracts, Copyrights, and Licensing, 9400 Southpark Center Loop, Orlando, Florida 32819-8647.

Printed in the U.S.A.

ISBN 978-0-544-26762-6

4 5 6 7 8 9 10   0982   22 21 20 19 18 17

4500658324   A B C D E F G

If you have received these materials as examination copies free of charge, Houghton Mifflin Harcourt Publishing Company retains title to the materials and they may not be resold. Resale of examination copies is strictly prohibited.

Possession of this publication in print format does not entitle users to convert this publication, or any portion of it, into electronic format.

Core Skills Social Studies
GRADE 4
Table of Contents

Introduction iv

Unit 1
Our Nation, the United States
Chapter 1 A Large and Varied Land 3
    Chapter Checkup 9
Chapter 2 Who Is an American? 10
    Chapter Checkup 15
Chapter 3 How Do Americans Live Together? 16
    Chapter Checkup 22
    Unit 1 Skill Builder Reading a Bar Graph 23
    Unit 1 Test 24

Unit 2
The Northeast Region
Chapter 4 Geography of the Northeast Region 25
    Chapter Checkup 29
Chapter 5 People of the Northeast Region 30
    Chapter Checkup 36
    Unit 2 Skill Builder Using a Distance Scale 37
    Unit 2 Test 38

Unit 3
The Southeast Region
Chapter 6 Geography of the Southeast Region 39
    Chapter Checkup 43
Chapter 7 People of the Southeast Region 44
    Chapter Checkup 51
    Unit 3 Skill Builder Reading a Table ... 52
    Unit 3 Activity Working a Puzzle 53
    Unit 3 Test 54

Unit 4
The North Central Region
Chapter 8 Geography of the North Central Region 55
    Chapter Checkup 59
Chapter 9 People of the North Central Region 60
    Chapter Checkup 67
    Unit 4 Skill Builder Planning Routes ... 68
    Unit 4 Test 69

Unit 5
The Rocky Mountain Region
Chapter 10 Geography of the Rocky Mountain Region 70
   Chapter Checkup..............................74
Chapter 11 People of the Rocky Mountain Region....................................75
   Chapter Checkup..............................82
   Unit 5 Skill Builder Reading a Line Graph.............................83
   Unit 5 Test..84

Unit 6
The Southwest Region
Chapter 12 Geography of the Southwest Region..85
   Chapter Checkup..............................88
Chapter 13 People of the Southwest Region..89
   Chapter Checkup..............................98
   Unit 6 Skill Builder Reading a Road Map............................99
   Unit 6 Test......................................100

Unit 7
The Pacific Region
Chapter 14 Geography of the Pacific Region..101
   Chapter Checkup............................107
Chapter 15 People of the Pacific Region..108
   Chapter Checkup............................116
   Unit 7 Skill Builder Learning from a Diagram.........................117
   Unit 7 Test......................................118

Map of the United States 119
Glossary 120
Answer Key...122

Introduction

Social studies focuses on developing knowledge and skill in history, geography, culture, economics, civics, and government. It also focuses on people and their interaction with each other and the world in which they live. *Core Skills: Social Studies* addresses these areas of study and correlates with national social studies curriculum. With this book, students can:

- gain a better understanding of their country and its regions
- practice map and geography skills
- work with charts and other graphic devices

The book features 15 chapter lessons on a variety of social studies topics. It also includes:

- interactive questions about the text or pictures
- chapter checkups
- unit skill builders to enhance social studies skills
- unit tests for each unit

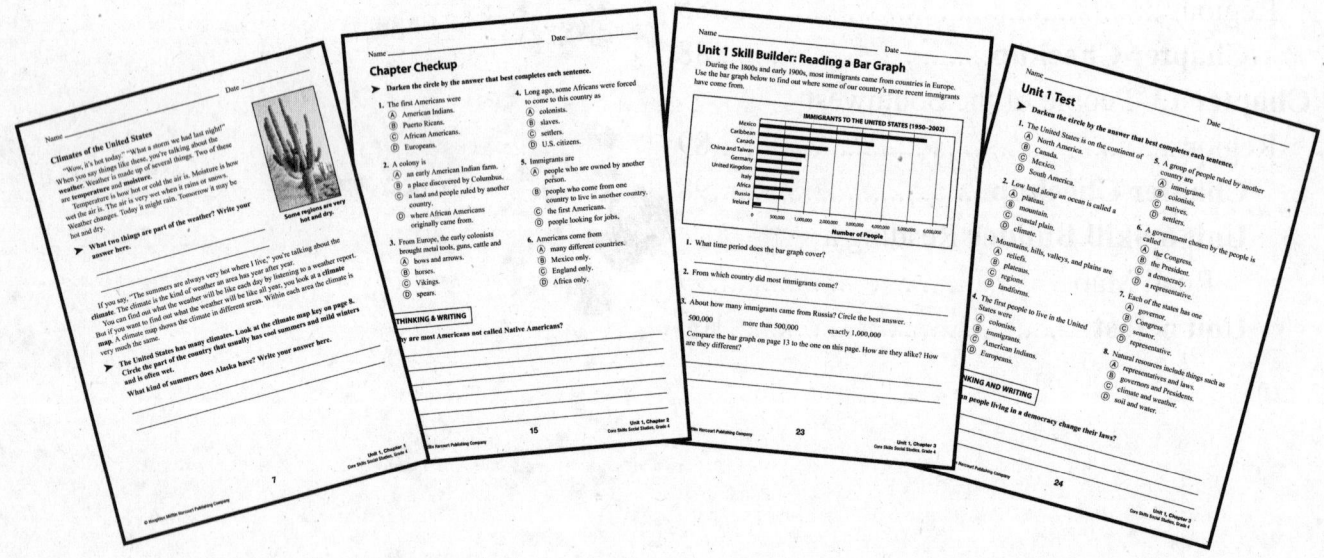

Name _____ Date _____

Chapter 1: A Large and Varied Land

Where is the United States? What does it look like? How hot or cold is it? These are questions about the **geography** of the United States. Geography is the study of Earth and how we live on it.

Where Is the United States?

The United States is on the **continent** of North America. A continent is a large body of land. The map on page 2 shows North America and the countries that are part of it.

The flag of the United States has one star for each state. How many stars are there?

▶ **Find the United States on the map on page 2. Write U.S. next to the United States. *U.S.* is the abbreviation for *United States*.**

Look at the map again. The United States looks like a puzzle with many pieces. These pieces are called **states**. There are 50 states. **United** means "together." The name of this country, the United States, means 50 states together.

Forty-eight states are in the part of the country that lies between Canada and Mexico. Each state touches at least one other state. Look at the map key. The dotted lines you see on the map stand for **borders**. Borders separate the states.

▶ **Look at the compass rose on the map on page 2. The letters *N*, *S*, *E*, and *W* stand for the four cardinal directions. They are North, South, East, and West. Put a ✔ on the country that borders the United States on the south.**

Name _____ Date _____

Two states do not touch any other state. They are Alaska and Hawaii. Hawaii is about 2,400 miles away in the Pacific Ocean.

➤ **Find Alaska on the map. What direction is Alaska from Mexico? Write your answer here.**

_____

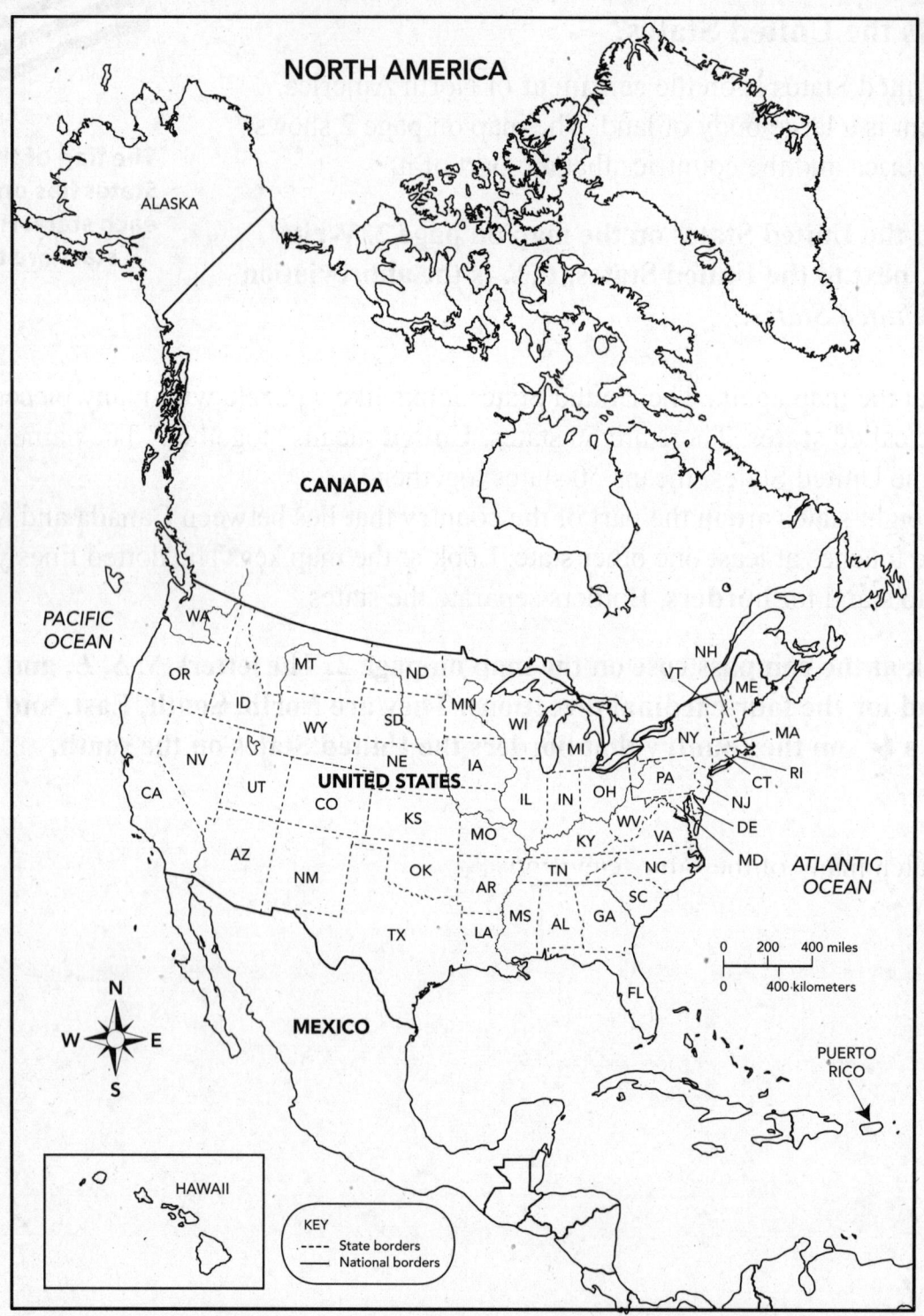

2

© Houghton Mifflin Harcourt Publishing Company

Unit 1, Chapter 1
Core Skills Social Studies, Grade 4

Name _____ Date _____

Regions of the United States

The United States is a very large country. In fact, it's the fourth-largest country in the world. This nation stretches 2,807 miles from the East Coast to the West Coast. And then there are Alaska and Hawaii, too! How can you study something so big?

One way to study this big nation is to divide it into areas called **regions**. The United States can be divided into six different regions:

- Northeast Region
- Southeast Region
- North Central Region
- Rocky Mountain Region
- Southwest Region
- Pacific Region

Some people live in a snowy region.

▶ Look at the region map on page 4. Find your state. Put a star on it.

What region is your state in? Write your answer here.

_____

Each region has something special about it. Some regions have lots of mountains, and some are very flat. Some regions get lots of rain, and some are very dry. Some regions are warm most of the year. Some regions get very cold in winter.

The regions of the United States can also be alike. Children in every region go to school. People watch many of the same television shows. They eat many of the same foods. And they do many of the same jobs.

▶ Look at the map on page 4. Find the region where you live. Color your region. Then choose five colors and shade the remaining five regions on the region map.

Name _____ Date _____

▶ **What do you think is one thing that makes your region special? Tell why. Write your answer here.**

_____

_____

_____

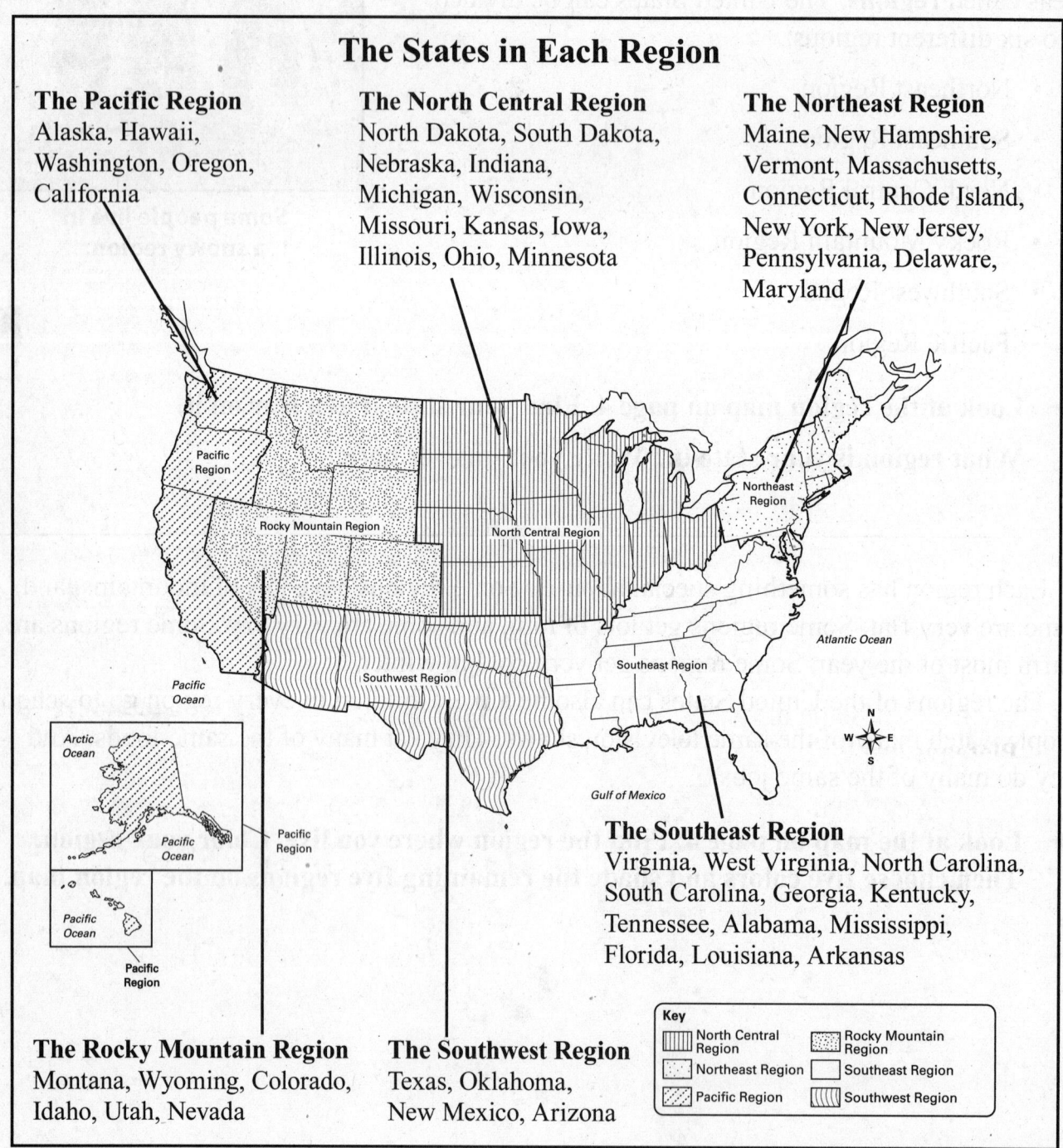

The States in Each Region

The Pacific Region
Alaska, Hawaii, Washington, Oregon, California

The North Central Region
North Dakota, South Dakota, Nebraska, Indiana, Michigan, Wisconsin, Missouri, Kansas, Iowa, Illinois, Ohio, Minnesota

The Northeast Region
Maine, New Hampshire, Vermont, Massachusetts, Connecticut, Rhode Island, New York, New Jersey, Pennsylvania, Delaware, Maryland

The Southeast Region
Virginia, West Virginia, North Carolina, South Carolina, Georgia, Kentucky, Tennessee, Alabama, Mississippi, Florida, Louisiana, Arkansas

The Rocky Mountain Region
Montana, Wyoming, Colorado, Idaho, Utah, Nevada

The Southwest Region
Texas, Oklahoma, New Mexico, Arizona

Name _____   Date _____

The Land of the United States

In some ways the land of the United States is like a giant roller coaster. A **physical map** shows where the land is high and where it is low. It can also show the shapes and names of rivers, lakes, deserts, plains, and mountains.

▶ **Look at the physical map on page 6. The shaded areas are mountains. What part of the country has more mountains, the East or the West? Write your answer here.**

_____

Mountains and hills and other shapes of the land are called **landforms**. The land along the ocean is a landform. It is called a **coast**. The coast along the Atlantic Ocean is a coastal **plain**. A plain is a low, flat area of land.

▶ **Look at the physical map key on page 6. Find the shading for plains. Find the plain that is on the East Coast of the United States. Mark an X on that plain. That X is the starting point for your roller-coaster ride across the United States!**

After the coastal plains, you slowly climb the Appalachian Mountains. Find the Appalachian Mountains on the map on page 6. Mark M on the mountains.

On the other side of the mountains are the plateaus. Plateaus are high, flat areas of land. Look at the map. Find the plateau near the Arkansas River. Put a P there.

Miles of wheat cover the Great Plains of the United States.

Plateaus are high, flat areas of land.

5

Unit 1, Chapter 1
Core Skills Social Studies, Grade 4

Name _____ Date _____

The roller coaster is zooming across the flat Great Plains. Get ready to climb the Rocky Mountains. They are some of the tallest mountains in the United States!

➤ **Mark another M on the Rocky Mountains.**

Next, you speed down the mountains and across a plateau. After the plateau, you climb more mountains until . . . splash! You're in the ocean!

➤ **Write the name of the ocean here.**

_____

_____

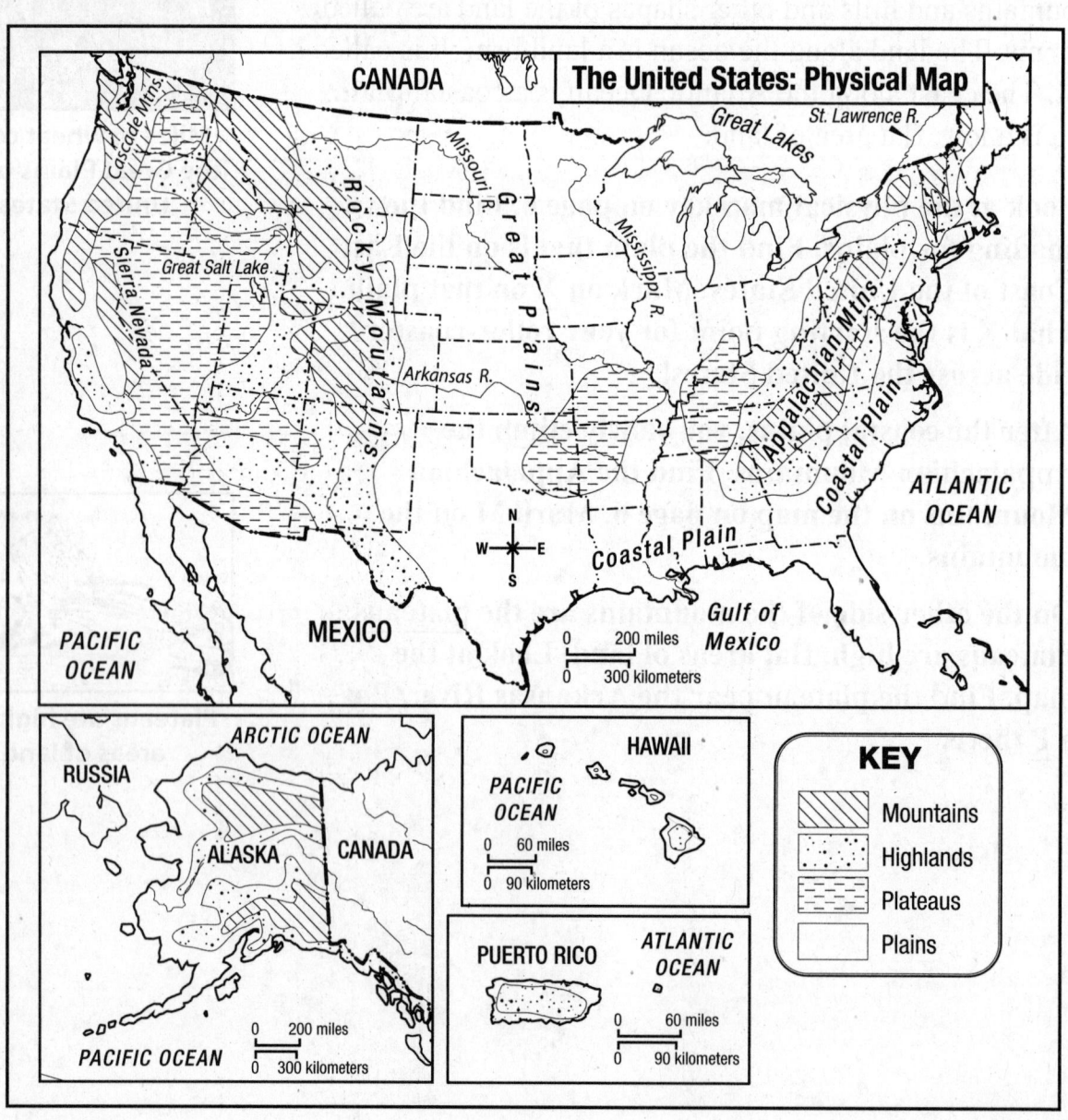

Unit 1, Chapter 1
© Houghton Mifflin Harcourt Publishing Company
Core Skills Social Studies, Grade 4

Climates of the United States

"Wow, it's hot today." "What a storm we had last night!" When you say things like these, you're talking about the **weather**. Weather is made up of several things. Two of these are **temperature** and **moisture**.

Temperature is how hot or cold the air is. Moisture is how wet the air is. The air is very wet when it rains or snows. Weather changes. Today it might rain. Tomorrow it may be hot and dry.

Some regions are very hot and dry.

▶ **What two things are part of the weather? Write your answer here.**

_____

_____

If you say, "The summers are always very hot where I live," you're talking about the **climate**. The climate is the kind of weather an area has year after year.

You can find out what the weather will be like each day by listening to a weather report. But if you want to find out what the weather will be like all year, you look at a **climate map**. A climate map shows the climate in different areas. Within each area the climate is very much the same.

▶ **The United States has many climates. Look at the climate map key on page 8. Circle the part of the country that usually has cool summers and mild winters and is often wet.**

What kind of summers does Alaska have? Write your answer here.

_____

_____

Name _____ Date _____

What kind of winters does Puerto Rico have? Write your answer here.

_____

_____

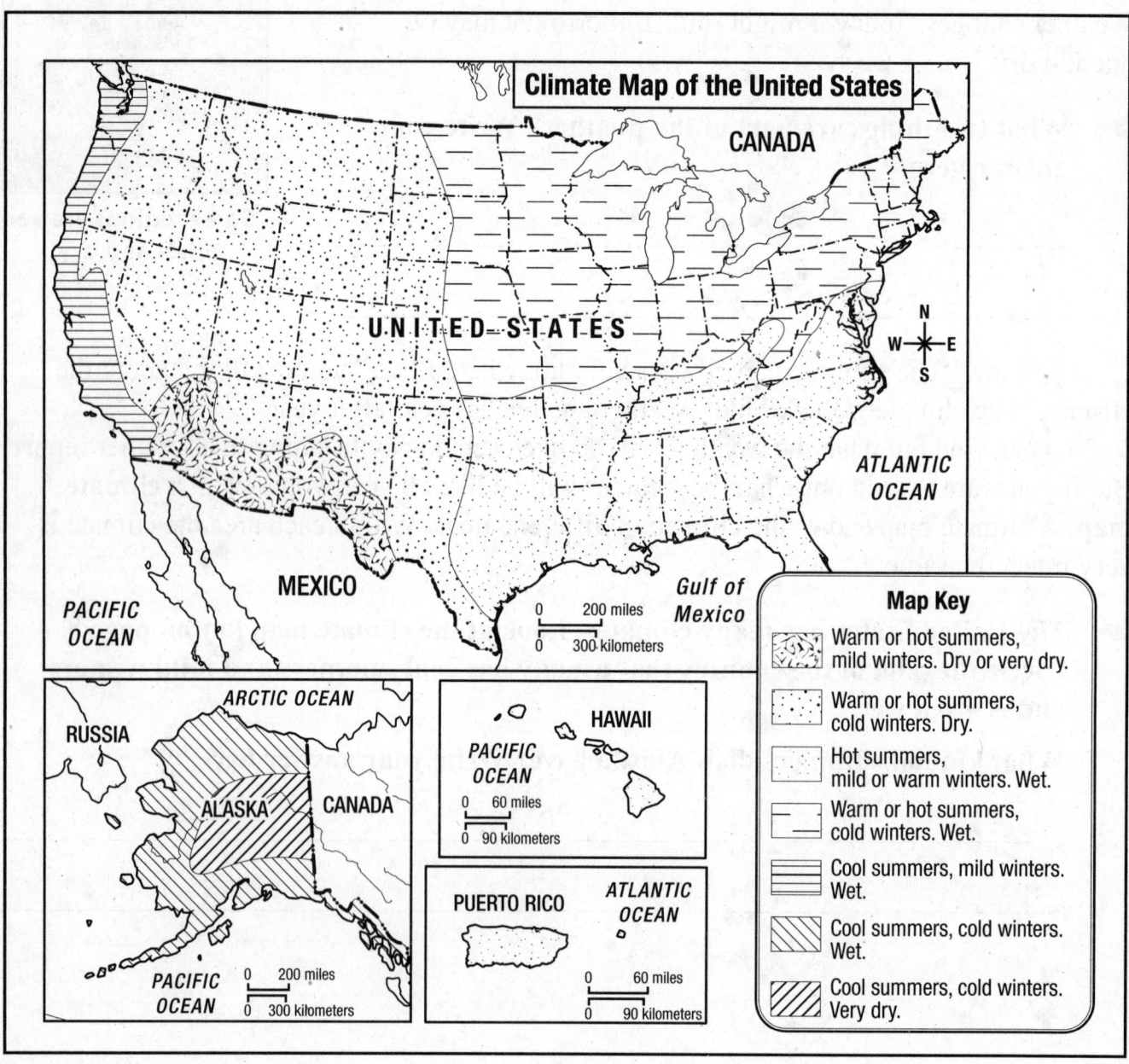

Name _____ Date _____

Chapter Checkup

▶ Darken the circle by the answer that best completes each sentence.

1. The United States has
   - Ⓐ 13 states.
   - Ⓑ 48 states.
   - Ⓒ 52 states.
   - Ⓓ 50 states.

2. Borders separate
   - Ⓐ continents.
   - Ⓑ landforms.
   - Ⓒ plains.
   - Ⓓ states and countries.

3. A region of the United States is
   - Ⓐ the study of Earth's land.
   - Ⓑ a large country.
   - Ⓒ a group of states.
   - Ⓓ a kind of weather.

4. A physical map shows
   - Ⓐ climate areas.
   - Ⓑ state borders.
   - Ⓒ where the land is high and low.
   - Ⓓ rivers only.

5. The land along the Atlantic Ocean is
   - Ⓐ a flat coastal plain.
   - Ⓑ a high plateau.
   - Ⓒ the Rocky Mountains.
   - Ⓓ Alaska.

6. A plateau is
   - Ⓐ low land along the ocean.
   - Ⓑ a tall mountain.
   - Ⓒ high, flat land.
   - Ⓓ a small island.

THINKING AND WRITING

How does it help to know what the weather will be like for the next few days?

_____
_____
_____
_____
_____
_____

Chapter 2: Who is an American?

Each person who lives in the United States is special in some way. We all live and work together in the United States. We are part of a special group—the American people.

The First Americans

The first people to live in the United States were **American Indians**, or **Native Americans**. *Native* means "the first people to live in a place." American Indians came from Asia to Alaska thousands of years ago. Over time, they settled all over North and South America.

The American Indians formed hundreds of different groups. Some groups of American Indians lived in small villages and planted crops such as squash, beans, and corn. Other groups traveled to find food and never stayed in one place for very long.

Some American Indians are skilled at weaving rugs.

▶ Where did American Indians who arrived in Alaska come from? Write your answer here.

_____

Name _____   Date _____

New Americans

The first explorers of North America were Vikings. They sailed from Greenland to North America about 1,000 years ago. They did not stay in North America. People in Europe, Asia, and Africa did not know that the Vikings had explored North America.

About 500 years after the Vikings explored North America, Christopher Columbus sailed west from Europe. He landed on an island between North and South America in 1492. Soon other explorers came from Europe.

Later, families from Europe started moving to North America, too. They began **colonies**. A colony is a group of people ruled by another country. The people living in the colonies had to work hard. These **colonists** built homes, farmed, and started businesses.

Homes in the early colonies looked like these homes. They were made of mud and sticks.

▶ Look at the picture graph below. Sometimes it is easier to understand numbers if you see them as pictures. This graph uses symbols for numbers. This picture graph shows how the colonies grew. How many colonists were there in 1680? How many were there in 1740, 60 years later? Write your answers here.

1680: _____   1740: _____

NUMBER OF COLONISTS IN THE 13 COLONIES (1680–1740)

1680	☺ ⸩
1700	☺ ☺ ⸩
1720	☺ ☺ ☺ ☺ ⸩
1740	☺ ☺ ☺ ☺ ☺ ☺ ☺ ☺

Each figure ☺ stands for 100,000 people.

Name _____ Date _____

New Americans Meet the First Americans

The colonists had come from farms, towns, and cities in Europe. North America was a wilderness area. The colonists had to learn new skills to live in North America. At first, most American Indians were friendly toward the colonists. American Indians taught the colonists about foods they could grow. From Europe, the colonists brought metal tools, guns, cattle, and horses. The American Indians had never seen such things before.

The Pilgrims were early colonists who learned skills from American Indians.

▶ **How did American Indians help the colonists? Write your answer here.**

_____

_____

_____

American Indians wanted to keep living on the land their people had lived on for hundreds of years. The colonists wanted to explore and use the land. They also wanted to build the kinds of towns and farms they remembered from Europe. American Indians and colonists fought many battles about land. The colonists fought with guns. The American Indians used spears and bows and arrows to fight the battles. Because their weapons were less powerful, many more American Indians died during the battles than colonists.

▶ **Why did the American Indians and the European colonists fight about how to use the land? Write your answer here.**

_____

_____

_____

More New Americans Arrive

Beginning in the 1600s, some Africans were forced to come to this country. These people were sold to colonists as **slaves**. A slave is a person who is owned by another person. Some colonists used slaves to do the hard work on the farms and in the new towns.

In 1861, Americans fought one another in the Civil War. After the war, slaves became free. New laws said that no person could ever be made a slave in the United States again.

During the 1700s and 1800s, many **immigrants** from Europe came to the United States. Immigrants are people who come from one country to live in another country. They wanted a chance to own land or find good jobs.

Today the largest numbers of immigrants come from Asia and Latin America. Today's immigrants, like immigrants of earlier times, hope to find a better life.

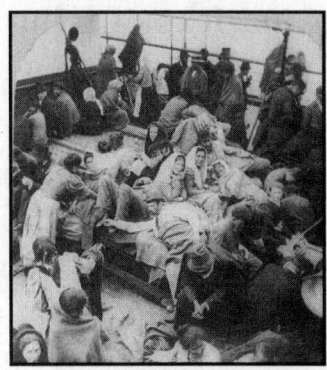

These immigrants from Europe arrived in New York City about 100 years ago.

▶ **A bar graph uses bars to stand for numbers. The bar graph below shows the countries that many immigrants came from between 1820 and 1950. Circle the name of the country the most immigrants came from.**

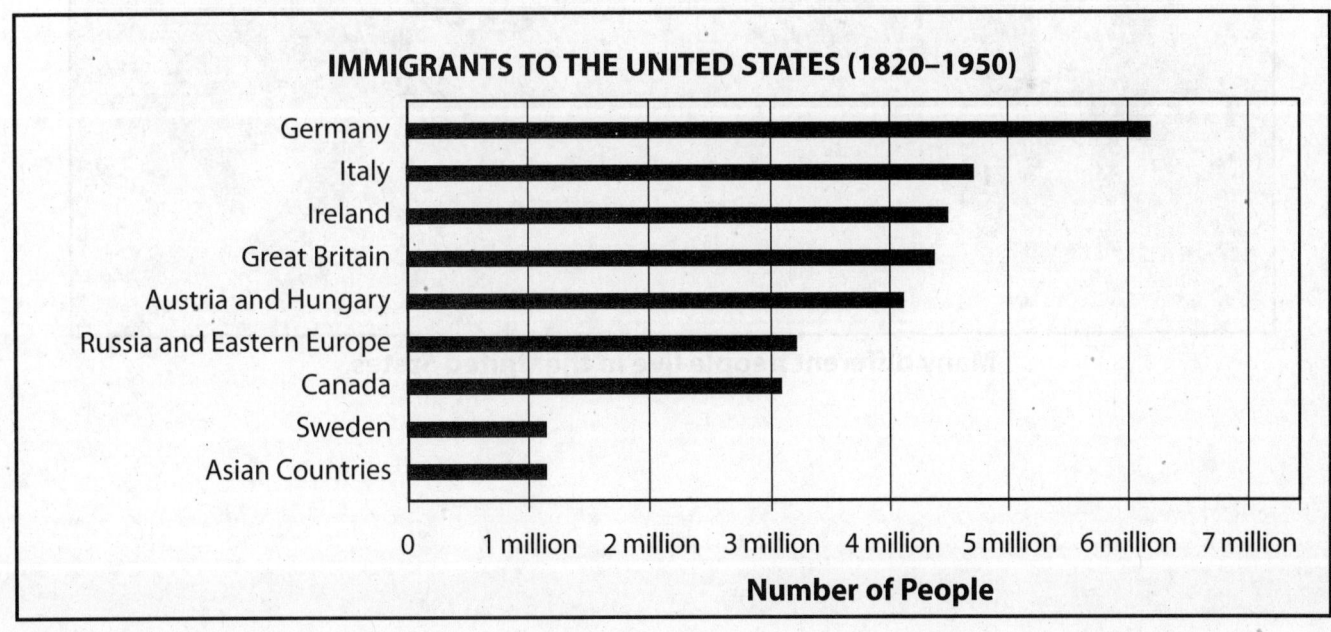

Americans Living Together

North Americans have many different backgrounds. Most Americans speak English, but some speak other languages, such as Spanish, Chinese, or Korean. In fact, many words you use each day come from other languages! Did you know that *banana* and *zebra* come from African languages? *Tomato* and *chipmunk* come from American Indian languages!

Although Americans are different in many ways, they are a lot alike. Many Americans enjoy the same foods, such as peanut butter and corn on the cob. Americans do many of the same things, such as play baseball and visit friends. Most importantly, Americans share the same home, the United States of America.

Many different people live in the United States.

Name _____ Date _____

Chapter Checkup

▶ **Darken the circle by the answer that best completes each sentence.**

1. The first Americans were
   - Ⓐ American Indians.
   - Ⓑ Puerto Ricans.
   - Ⓒ African Americans.
   - Ⓓ Europeans.

2. A colony is
   - Ⓐ an early American Indian farm.
   - Ⓑ a place discovered by Columbus.
   - Ⓒ a land and people ruled by another country.
   - Ⓓ where African Americans originally came from.

3. From Europe, the early colonists brought metal tools, guns, cattle and
   - Ⓐ bows and arrows.
   - Ⓑ horses.
   - Ⓒ Vikings.
   - Ⓓ spears.

4. Long ago, some Africans were forced to come to this country as
   - Ⓐ colonists.
   - Ⓑ slaves.
   - Ⓒ settlers.
   - Ⓓ U.S. citizens.

5. Immigrants are
   - Ⓐ people who are owned by another person.
   - Ⓑ people who come from one country to live in another country.
   - Ⓒ the first Americans.
   - Ⓓ people looking for jobs.

6. Americans come from
   - Ⓐ many different countries.
   - Ⓑ Mexico only.
   - Ⓒ England only.
   - Ⓓ Africa only.

THINKING AND WRITING

Why are most Americans not called Native Americans?

_____
_____
_____
_____

Name _____ Date _____

Chapter 3: How Do Americans Live Together?

In the last chapter you read about the many kinds of people who have come to live in the United States. Did you wonder how so many different people can live in one country?

Our Nation's Leaders

It isn't easy for people with different ideas to work and live together. Imagine how hard it would be to drive a car if everyone did what he or she wanted to do. Some people might drive on the right, and some might drive on the left. Some people might even drive on the sidewalks. That's why we have rules to tell drivers where they can drive.

➤ **Write one thing that might happen if there were no rules for people who drive cars. Write your answer here.**

_____

_____

This police officer is talking to students about obeying laws.

Name _____ Date _____

Towns, states, and nations need rules, too. Who makes these rules? Groups of people called **governments** do. Rules made by governments are called **laws**. Governments also make sure that the laws are obeyed. We have governments for our towns, our states, and our nation.

A town or city government is called a **local government**. Local governments provide **services** such as the police, who work to help and protect us.

➤ **Look at the picture below. Local governments provide this service. Write the reason why this service is important to you.**

_____

_____

Your state government provides services for all the communities in your state. It builds roads between cities. It makes laws about what people can and cannot do in the state.

The government of the United States also makes laws and provides services. For example, it helps maintain highways between states.

Firefighting is a local service. Firefighters must be near homes and businesses.

Name _____ Date _____

The United States is a **democracy**. That means that the people who live here can **vote** for, or choose, the people in their governments. The people who live in a town vote for the **mayor** of the town. The mayor is the person who leads the town.

The people who live in a state vote for the **governor**. The governor is the person who leads the state. The person who leads the whole country is called the **President**. Almost everyone who is 18 or older can vote to choose the President.

The Capitol building in Washington, D.C.

▶ **Circle the name of the person who leads the United States.**

    mayor   governor   President

The President leads the country but does not make the laws. The people who make the country's laws are in **Congress**. Congress has two parts: the **Senate** and the **House of Representatives**.

The people of each state vote for two senators. They also vote for the representatives. The more people there are in a state, the more representatives the state has. Vermont has very few people, so it has only one representative. California has lots of people, so it has 53 representatives.

It is very hard to lead a town, state, or country. It is also hard to make good laws. That is why people have to be very careful when they vote. We must try to pick the best people to be our leaders.

▶ **If you were in Congress, what law would you like to make? Write it here.**

_____

_____

Name _____ Date _____

Building a Nation

For hundreds of years, people in the United States have worked hard to build homes and businesses.

Farming has always been important. Many American Indians and colonists were farmers. Today American farms grow food for people in the United States and other countries.

People still make some things, such as quilts, by hand.

Americans also make a lot of goods. American Indians and early colonists made their own goods by hand. In the 1800s, Americans began making goods in factories.

The way Americans work today is very different from colonial times. Americans have all kinds of jobs. The bar graph on this page shows different job groupings. It also shows how many people work in each job grouping. Today, the **service job** grouping has the largest number of people. People who have service jobs do not *make* anything. People who have service jobs do something to help other people. Service workers might give you a haircut, serve you food, or clean your teeth.

➤ Look at the bar graph. Which job group has about twice as many workers as the construction group?

_____

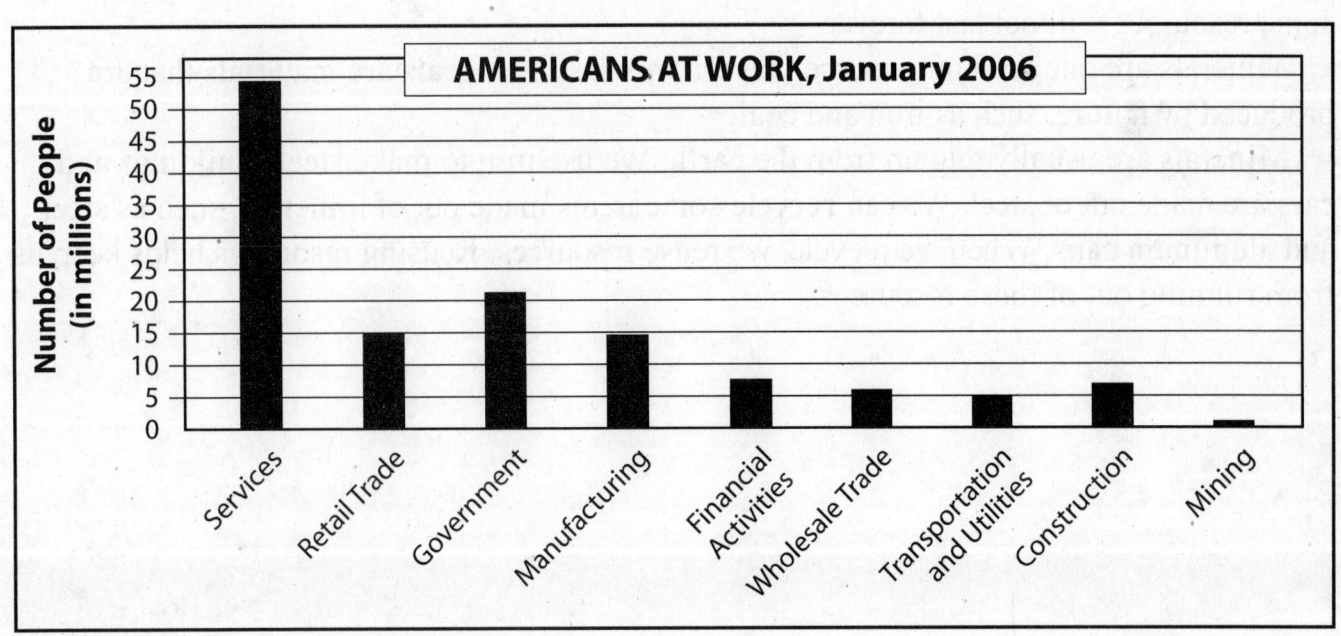

Our Natural Resources

The United States is rich in **natural resources**. Natural resources have helped make our country great. A natural resource is something from nature that we use.

One of the most important resources of the United States is soil. Soil is used to grow crops. Water is another important resource. You probably never realized how important water is. It's so easy to get a glass of water. But if we didn't have much water, we couldn't grow enough food.

➤ **Write two ways you use water.**

_____

_____

Water and trees are two important resources.

Water is useful for other things, too. We use our lakes and rivers to get to places and to move things. Many of our crops and products travel on ships. We also use the power of moving water to make electricity.

When the colonists came from Europe, there were many natural resources. Most people thought the United States had more than enough natural resources. Today we know that some resources will not last forever.

Minerals are one kind of resource that will not last. **Minerals** are materials that are produced by nature, such as iron and coal.

Minerals are usually dug up from the earth. We use iron to make steel. Buildings and cars are made out of steel. We can **recycle** some items made out of minerals, such as steel and aluminum cans. When we recycle, we reuse resources. Reusing resources helps keep us from running out of those resources.

Trees are another great resource. We use them to build homes and furniture. Paper is also made from trees. Before the colonists came, there were forests all over North America. Many forests have been cut down since then. Luckily, trees can be replanted. We have to be careful how many trees we use because trees take a long time to grow.

People can save trees by recycling paper. By recycling paper, we reuse the paper and do not have to cut down as many trees.

➤ **What do we know today about natural resources that the colonists didn't know?**

_____

_____

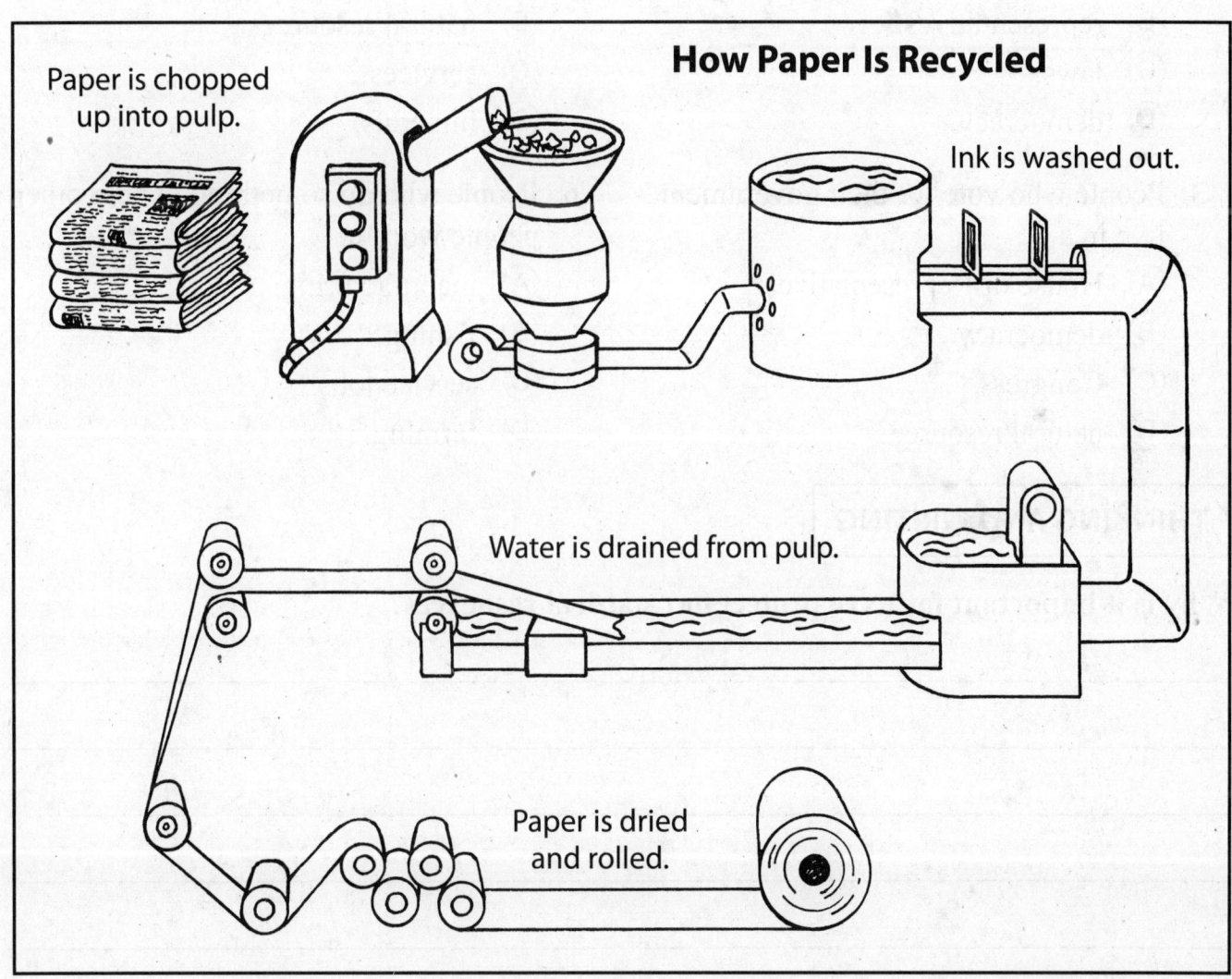

How Paper Is Recycled

Paper is chopped up into pulp.

Ink is washed out.

Water is drained from pulp.

Paper is dried and rolled.

Name _____ Date _____

Chapter Checkup

▶ **Darken the circle by the answer that best completes each sentence.**

1. A group of people who make laws and provide services is called
   - Ⓐ a business.
   - Ⓑ a government.
   - Ⓒ a democracy.
   - Ⓓ a mayor.

2. Rules made by governments are called
   - Ⓐ voters.
   - Ⓑ representatives.
   - Ⓒ laws.
   - Ⓓ democracy.

3. People who vote for their government live in a
   - Ⓐ House of Representatives.
   - Ⓑ democracy.
   - Ⓒ Congress.
   - Ⓓ natural resource.

4. The person who leads a state is called the
   - Ⓐ Senate.
   - Ⓑ Mayor.
   - Ⓒ President.
   - Ⓓ Governor.

5. Soil, water, and forests are all
   - Ⓐ climates.
   - Ⓑ natural resources.
   - Ⓒ services.
   - Ⓓ minerals.

6. People who do something to help other people work in
   - Ⓐ manufacturing.
   - Ⓑ fishing.
   - Ⓒ service jobs.
   - Ⓓ farming.

THINKING AND WRITING

Why is it important for us to protect our natural resources?

_____
_____
_____
_____
_____

Name _____ Date _____

Unit 1 Skill Builder: Reading a Bar Graph

During the 1800s and early 1900s, most immigrants came from countries in Europe. Use the bar graph below to find out where some of our country's more recent immigrants have come from.

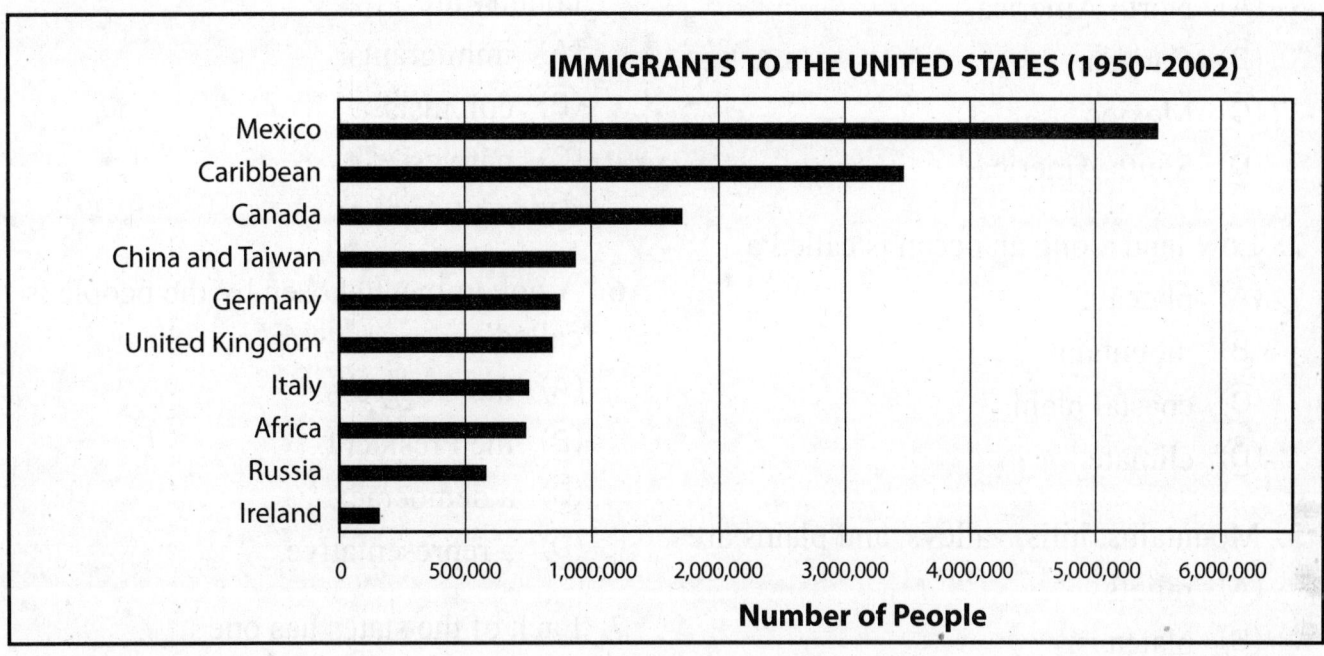

1. What time period does the bar graph cover?

   _____

2. From which country did most immigrants come?

   _____

3. About how many immigrants came from Russia? Circle the best answer.

   500,000   more than 500,000   exactly 1,000,000

4. Compare the bar graph on page 13 to the one on this page. How are they alike? How are they different?

   _____

   _____

Name _____ Date _____

Unit 1 Test

➤ **Darken the circle by the answer that best completes each sentence.**

1. The United States is on the continent of
   - Ⓐ North America.
   - Ⓑ Canada.
   - Ⓒ Mexico.
   - Ⓓ South America.

2. Low land along an ocean is called a
   - Ⓐ plateau.
   - Ⓑ mountain.
   - Ⓒ coastal plain.
   - Ⓓ climate.

3. Mountains, hills, valleys, and plains are
   - Ⓐ reliefs.
   - Ⓑ plateaus.
   - Ⓒ regions.
   - Ⓓ landforms.

4. The first people to live in the United States were
   - Ⓐ colonists.
   - Ⓑ immigrants.
   - Ⓒ American Indians.
   - Ⓓ Europeans.

5. A group of people ruled by another country are
   - Ⓐ immigrants.
   - Ⓑ colonists.
   - Ⓒ natives.
   - Ⓓ settlers.

6. A government chosen by the people is called
   - Ⓐ the Congress.
   - Ⓑ the President.
   - Ⓒ a democracy.
   - Ⓓ a representative.

7. Each of the states has one
   - Ⓐ governor.
   - Ⓑ Congress.
   - Ⓒ senator.
   - Ⓓ representative.

8. Natural resources include things such as
   - Ⓐ representatives and laws.
   - Ⓑ governors and Presidents.
   - Ⓒ climate and weather.
   - Ⓓ soil and water.

THINKING AND WRITING

How can people living in a democracy change their laws?

_____

_____

Name _____   Date _____

Chapter 4: Geography of the Northeast Region

You may already know something about the geography of the Northeast Region. You know where this region is in the United States. Its name tells where it is.

States and Cities

There are 11 states in the Northeast Region. Look at the map below. Put your finger on each of the named states.

➤ **Find the state in the Northeast Region that is the farthest north. Write N on that state.**

Find the state that is the farthest south. Write S on that state.

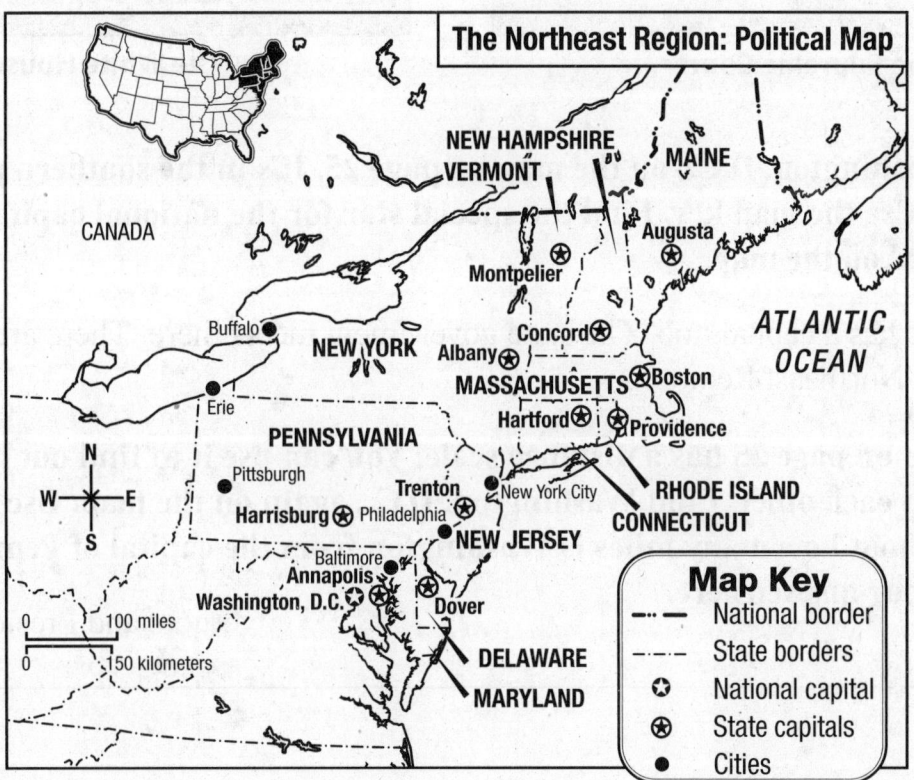

Name _____ Date _____

A **capital** is a city where a government meets. Washington, D.C., is the capital of our country. It is in the Northeast Region. Washington, D.C., is not like any other city in the United States. It's in a special place called the District of Columbia. We shorten *District of Columbia* to *D.C.*

The Supreme Court

The White House

➤ **Find Washington, D.C., on the map on page 25. It's in the southern part of the region. Use the map key. Find the special star for the national capital. Circle the same star on the map.**

Every state has a capital, too. The state government meets there. There are 11 state capitals in the Northeast Region.

➤ **The map on page 25 has a distance scale. You can use it to find out how far places are from each other. Find Washington, D.C., again on the map. Use the distance scale. About how many miles is Washington from the capital of Pennsylvania? Write your answer here.**

_____

Name _____   Date _____

The Land and Water

Pretend that you are planning a bike trip in the Northeast Region. You're going to start on the coast of Maine. Remember, the coast is where the land is next to the ocean. Look at the map and the map key below. Find the plains. Biking is easy on the flat plains along the coast!

There are **highlands** west of the coast. Highlands are hilly areas between flat lands and mountains. Biking will be hard in the highlands.

➤ **Find the shading for highlands in the map key. Draw lines from the key to three highland areas.**

On the map there is shading for the mountains. Circle the Appalachian Mountains. (Remember, *Mtns.* is short for *Mountains*.) Here biking will really be hard!

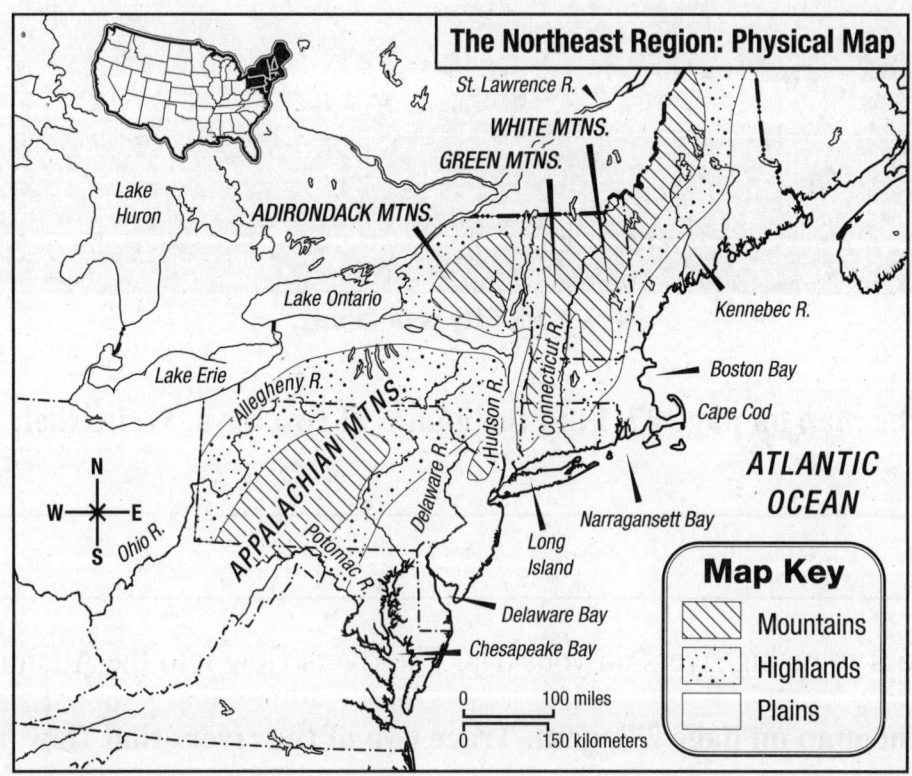

27

Unit 2, Chapter 4
© Houghton Mifflin Harcourt Publishing Company
Core Skills Social Studies, Grade 4

You're going to see a lot of water on your trip through the Northeast. Along the coast you will see some large **bays**. A bay is a place where the water is almost surrounded by land. On a map, a bay looks a little like someone has taken a bite out of the coast.

Bays make safe **harbors** for ships because the water is protected by land. New York and Boston are two big cities that are on bays. These cities are **ports**. A port is a place where people can load and unload ships.

Bay

New York City is on a bay.

▶ **Look at the map on page 27. Find the names of two bays. Write their names here.**

_____

_____

You will cross some big rivers on your trip. The rivers flow into the Atlantic Ocean.

▶ **Look at the map on page 27 again. Trace two of the rivers that flow into the ocean.**

Name _____ Date _____

Chapter Checkup

▶ **Darken the circle by the answer that best completes each sentence.**

1. Two of the states in the Northeast Region are
   - Ⓐ Virginia and Georgia.
   - Ⓑ New York and Pennsylvania.
   - Ⓒ Kansas and Nebraska.
   - Ⓓ California and Hawaii.

2. A capital is
   - Ⓐ a place where ships are unloaded.
   - Ⓑ a city where a government meets.
   - Ⓒ a large river.
   - Ⓓ near the ocean.

3. Washington, D.C., is
   - Ⓐ the capital of the United States.
   - Ⓑ the capital of Maine.
   - Ⓒ the capital of New York.
   - Ⓓ the capital of Washington.

4. The land along the coast of the Northeast is
   - Ⓐ flat.
   - Ⓑ hilly.
   - Ⓒ filled with mountains.
   - Ⓓ a highland.

5. Places that make safe harbors for ships are
   - Ⓐ capitals.
   - Ⓑ highlands.
   - Ⓒ bays.
   - Ⓓ mountains.

6. In a port, people
   - Ⓐ live very close to mountains.
   - Ⓑ load and unload ships.
   - Ⓒ work on farms.
   - Ⓓ get on trains.

THINKING AND WRITING

Pretend that you could live any place in the Northeast. Where would you like to live? Why?

_____

_____

_____

_____

Name _____ Date _____

Chapter 5: People of the Northeast Region

The Northeast Region is not just bays, mountains, and big cities. In this chapter you'll learn about the people of the Northeast. Let's begin by visiting the Northeast in the early 1600s, over 400 years ago.

Long Ago: The Pilgrims

"Land ho!" a sailor shouted. The people in the little ship looked through the fog. They saw land! These tired people had left England two months before. They had sailed through many storms. At times, they thought their ship, the *Mayflower*, was going to sink. Now, on November 20, 1620, they had finished their trip across the Atlantic Ocean.

Pilgrims traveled on the *Mayflower*.

We call these people the Pilgrims. They left England because the laws there allowed only one religion. The Pilgrims wanted to practice their own religion.

So the Pilgrims started a colony in North America. There they built their own church and their own school. They called their new town Plymouth, after the city that had been their home in England.

➤ **Why did the Pilgrims leave England? Write your answer here.**

_____

_____

_____

Name _____ Date _____

The Pilgrims had many problems that first winter. They had little food, and it was too late in the season to plant crops. It was very cold. Almost half the Pilgrims died that winter. The others thought about going back to England.

➤ **How did the climate affect the Pilgrims? Write your answer here.**

_____

_____

_____

The Pilgrims were saved by the American Indians who lived near Plymouth. American Indians had lived there for hundreds of years. They knew how to grow and find food. An American Indian named Squanto taught the Pilgrims how to plant corn, catch fish, and even get maple syrup from trees.

American Indians helped the Pilgrims grow crops.

➤ **Why did the American Indians know more about getting food than the Pilgrims? Write your answer here.**

_____

_____

_____

When spring came, the Pilgrims planted corn and other crops. By the end of the summer, they had a lot of food. They decided to celebrate by having a feast with their new friends.

Before the meal, the Pilgrims gave thanks for the good harvest and for the help the American Indians gave them. They gave thanks for being alive in a new land.

This feast was the first Thanksgiving. Many years later, Thanksgiving became a holiday for everyone in the United States.

Where Do People Live in the Northeast Region?

The Pilgrims were some of the first people to move from their country to North America. But over the years, people came to the Northeast from countries around the world. Today more than 65 million people live in the Northeast.

Most people in the Northeast live in cities. Look at the map of the Northeast on page 25. Find Boston, Massachusetts. Then find Washington, D.C. Imagine a straight line between them. If you rode along that line in a car, you would be in cities most of the time.

Many people ride the subway in New York City.

► **Let's see how far away from each other Boston and Washington, D.C., really are. Use the distance scale on the map on page 25. Measure the distance in miles between these two cities. Write the distance here.**

_____

Many people in the Northeast live in **suburbs**. Suburbs are towns or small cities near big cities. Many people who live in suburbs work in the city.

People would have to live very close to their jobs if there was no **transportation**. Transportation is the way people travel to places. People drive on highways or take buses or trains.

► **What kinds of transportation do you use in your community? Write your answer here.**

_____

_____

You remember that the Pilgrims began a community called Plymouth. Boston, Massachusetts, is a city near Plymouth. Boston was started by other people soon after the Pilgrims came to Plymouth. Look at the picture of Boston at the top of page 33.

Name _____ Date _____

Boston, Massachusetts

Today, Boston is much bigger than Plymouth. One reason Boston is big is that it is by a large bay. Boston is on a river, too. The people who started Boston shipped many goods to England. Boston soon became an important port. Boston is the capital of Massachusetts. Three other port cities in the Northeast are also state capitals.

▶ **Look back at the map on page 25. Can you find the capital cities that are also ports? Write their names here.**

_____, Rhode Island

_____, Delaware

_____, Maryland

One of the most important cities in the region is Baltimore, Maryland. Baltimore is a very old and busy port. Tourists like to visit parts of the old harbor. One area is called Harborplace. People go there to shop and to eat. The National Aquarium is nearby.

Philadelphia, Pennsylvania, is one of the oldest cities in the United States. It was started by William Penn more than 300 years ago. Penn's colonists left England so they could practice their own religion.

▶ **How were the colonists of Plymouth and Philadelphia alike? Write your answer here.**

_____

_____

Look at the picture of Independence Hall on this page. It is in Philadelphia. More than 200 years ago, people from all the colonies met there. On July 4, 1776, they decided to start a new country. Many people visit Independence Hall every year.

Working in the Northeast Region

The resources of a region create many jobs. Crops need to be harvested. Trees need to be cut and planted. Food needs to be made. One of the most important resources of the Northeast is the Atlantic Ocean.

➤ **There are 11 states in the Northeast. Look at the map on page 25. Count the states that are next to the ocean. Write the answer here.**

Independence Hall in Philadelphia, Pennsylvania

Can you guess why the Atlantic Ocean is such an important resource? One reason is that it's full of fish!

Early every morning, fishing boats leave the ports of the Northeast. They come back with thousands of fish. The fish are sold to stores all over the Northeast and in other regions.

Most people in the Northeast do not work on fishing boats. Many people have service jobs. Remember that service jobs are jobs that help other people. People who work in stores, offices, and restaurants have service jobs. Firefighters, police officers, and teachers are service workers, too.

➤ **How does a firefighter help people?**

Fishing boats in Maine

Name _____ Date _____

Some service jobs in the Northeast help people in other regions of the country. One of these jobs is television news. Television companies have news offices in the Northeast. These offices get reports from around the world. They show news programs that are seen all over the country.

The Pilgrims had to wait many months for a ship to come with news from England. Today's television news programs can show us things as they happen.

Television is one part of a business that is called the communications business. To **communicate** means "to share information." One way people communicate is by talking. Newspapers share news and other information with many people. In fact, any way that news or information goes from one person or place to another is a way of communicating.

Today, many people use computers to communicate. Office workers can use computers to send electronic mail, or e-mail, to other workers who are far away. E-mail is a very quick way of communicating information.

▶ **Write two ways you communicate.**

_____

_____

Manufacturing also provides jobs for many people in the Northeast. People manufacture, or make, all kinds of goods. In the Northeast, most of the goods they make are small, like clocks and books. But there are some companies that make airplanes and other big machines.

Textiles—making thread, yarn, and cloth—has long been an important industry in the region. Thousands of miles of thread are made in factories every day. The thread will be woven into cloth.

Name _____ Date _____

Chapter Checkup

▶ **Darken the circle by the answer that best completes each sentence.**

1. The Pilgrims came to the Northeast to
   - Ⓐ learn to plant corn.
   - Ⓑ be free to practice their religion.
   - Ⓒ meet American Indians.
   - Ⓓ find New York.

2. Many people in the Northeast live in
   - Ⓐ villages.
   - Ⓑ colonies.
   - Ⓒ bays.
   - Ⓓ suburbs.

3. Buses, trains, and cars are types of
   - Ⓐ communication.
   - Ⓑ transportation.
   - Ⓒ manufacturing.
   - Ⓓ service jobs.

4. Boston and New York City are
   - Ⓐ on the Pacific Ocean.
   - Ⓑ state capitals.
   - Ⓒ important port cities.
   - Ⓓ on the same river.

5. An important resource of the Northeast Region is
   - Ⓐ the Atlantic Ocean.
   - Ⓑ television news.
   - Ⓒ Independence Hall.
   - Ⓓ clothing.

6. When you communicate, you
   - Ⓐ make goods.
   - Ⓑ start colonies.
   - Ⓒ use a computer.
   - Ⓓ share information.

THINKING AND WRITING

Why was it important to the Pilgrims for Squanto to teach them how to plant corn and catch fish?

_____
_____
_____
_____
_____

Name _____   Date _____

Unit 2 Skill Builder: Using a Distance Scale

In this unit you learned about Washington, D.C., the capital of the United States. Suppose you visited Washington. You would probably want to visit some of the city's famous places. Use the map and the distance scale to find out the distances between some of the places you could visit.

1. Find the White House on the map. Then find the Capitol. How many miles is the White House from the Capitol? _____

2. Suppose that after you visited the Capitol, you visited the Library of Congress. About how many kilometers would you travel? _____

3. How many kilometers from each other are the Library of Congress and the Lincoln Memorial? _____

4. The Washington Monument and the Smithsonian Institution look close to each other on the map. What is the real distance in miles between them?

_____

Name _____ Date _____

Unit 2 Test

➤ **Darken the circle by the answer that best completes each sentence.**

1. The eastern part of the Northeast Region is along the
    - Ⓐ Pacific Ocean.
    - Ⓑ Rocky Mountains.
    - Ⓒ Atlantic Ocean.
    - Ⓓ Gulf of Mexico.

2. The capital of the United States is
    - Ⓐ New York City.
    - Ⓑ Washington, D.C.
    - Ⓒ Plymouth.
    - Ⓓ Boston, Massachusetts.

3. The hilly areas between flat lands and mountains are called
    - Ⓐ plains.
    - Ⓑ coast.
    - Ⓒ highlands.
    - Ⓓ plateaus.

4. Water that is almost completely surrounded by land is called
    - Ⓐ an ocean.
    - Ⓑ a port.
    - Ⓒ a province.
    - Ⓓ a bay.

5. A city where ships are loaded and unloaded is a
    - Ⓐ port.
    - Ⓑ harbor.
    - Ⓒ capital.
    - Ⓓ suburb.

6. The bays, harbors, and ports in the Northeast are important for
    - Ⓐ communication.
    - Ⓑ service jobs.
    - Ⓒ shipping materials and products.
    - Ⓓ suburbs.

7. The Pilgrims began a community called
    - Ⓐ Boston.
    - Ⓑ Plymouth.
    - Ⓒ Baltimore.
    - Ⓓ Philadelphia.

8. Teachers and firefighters have
    - Ⓐ manufacturing jobs.
    - Ⓑ transportation jobs.
    - Ⓒ service jobs.
    - Ⓓ harbor jobs.

THINKING AND WRITING

Why do you think many early cities in North America began as port cities?

_____

_____

Name _____   Date _____

Chapter 6: Geography of the Southeast Region

Welcome to the Southeast Region! It's a land of long, hot summers and mild winters. It's a land of wide plains, rolling hills, and tall mountains.

Where Is the Southeast Region?

There are 12 states in the Southeast Region. Put your finger on each of the labeled states on the map below.

➤ Write an S on the state that is farthest south. Write an N on the state that is farthest north.

Name _____   Date _____

Like the states of the Northeast Region, many states in the Southeast Region are next to the Atlantic Ocean.

➤ **Look at the map on page 39. Find the states that are next to the Atlantic Ocean. Circle the names of those states.**

The southern part of the Southeast Region is near the Gulf of Mexico. Like a bay, a **gulf** is a large body of water that joins an ocean. It is partly surrounded by land. Find the Gulf of Mexico on the map.

Certain kinds of bad weather begin over large bodies of water. A **hurricane** is a storm with very strong winds and heavy rain. Some hurricanes start over the Gulf of Mexico and the Atlantic Ocean. Some hit the coast of the Southeast. Hurricanes can kill people. They can destroy buildings and crops.

➤ **Look at this table about hurricanes. A <u>table</u> lists facts so you can compare them easily. Which hurricane caused the most damage? Write the name of the hurricane and the year here.**

_____

Hurricanes of the Southeast

Name of Hurricane	Year	States Hardest Hit by Hurricane	Cost of Damage
Katrina	2005	Louisiana Alabama Mississippi	$200,000,000,000
Andrew	1992	Florida Louisiana	$7,250,000,000
Hugo	1989	South Carolina	$7,000,000,000
Frederic	1979	Alabama Mississippi	$2,250,000,000
Camille	1969	Mississippi Louisiana Alabama	$1,500,000,000

Name _____ Date _____

What Is the Land Like?

If you took a bike trip in the Southeast, you would have lots of flat plains to ride on. The plains near the Atlantic Ocean are called the Coastal Plain because they are near the coast. They have good soil and lots of water.

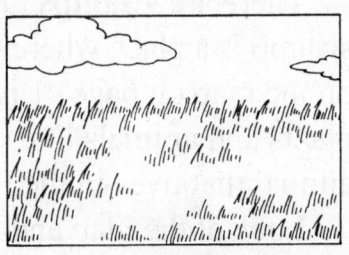
Plains

▶ Put your pencil on the plains at the upper right part of this map. Trace a bike route as far south as you can. Make an X where you stop.

Find the Savannah River. Suppose you decide to ride northwest along the river. Look at the map key. Would riding your bike get harder or easier? Why? Write your answer here.

_____

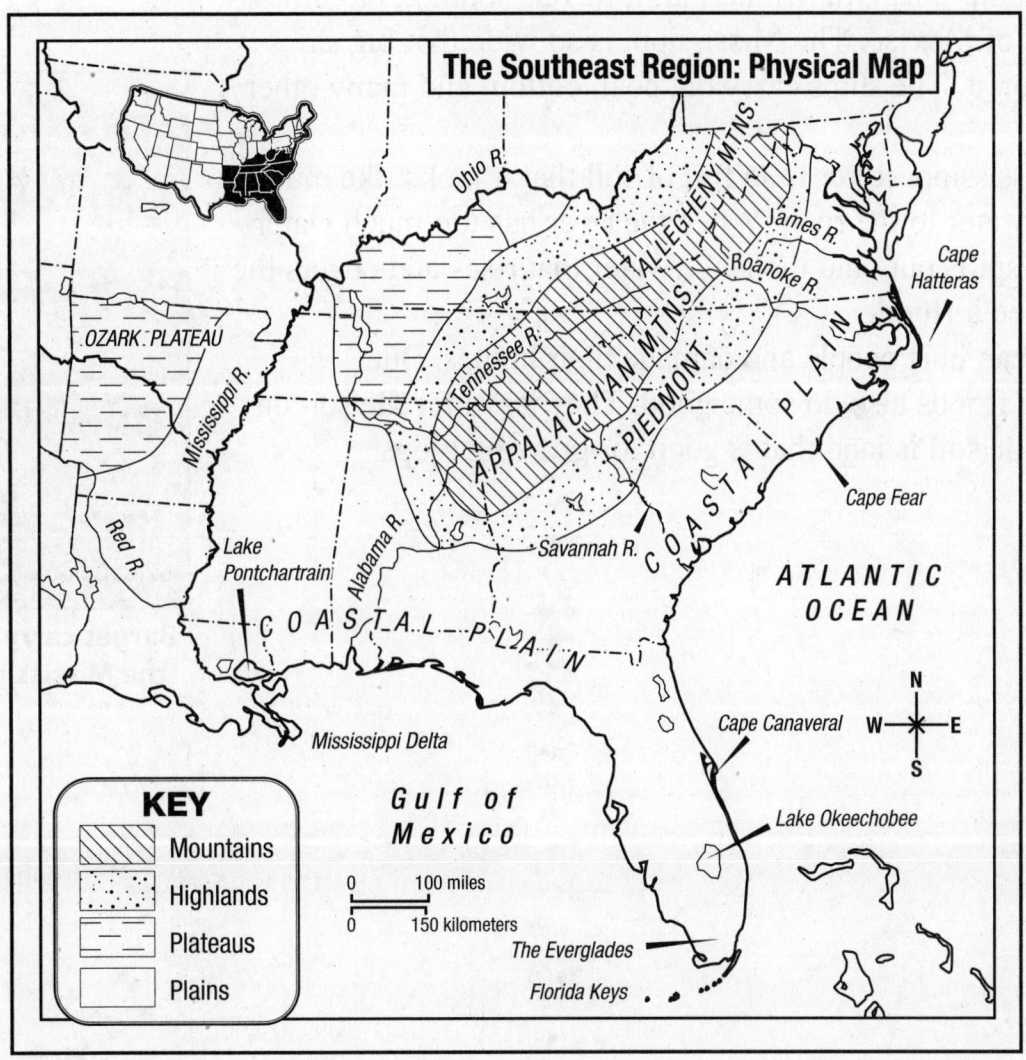

There are **swamps** in some parts of the Coastal Plain. A swamp is a place where the land is always wet. The X you made on the map on page 41 is near the Everglades swamp. Many plants and animals live in swamps. Alligators are one kind of animal that lives in the Everglades.

Look at the map and map key on page 41. Find the mountains. They are called the Appalachian Mountains.

➤ **Now look at the western part of the map. What is the longest river you see? Write your answer here.**

_____

The Mississippi River runs through the western plains of the region. It is the second-longest river in the United States. This river begins far north, in Minnesota. It travels south 2,340 miles to the Gulf of Mexico. The Mississippi is so wide that big ships can travel on it. The ships carry oil, coal, cotton, and many other products.

The Mississippi River is so full of soil that it looks like mud. Rains add water to the river. When the river has too much water in it, some spills out onto the land. Water that rises and covers the land is called a **flood**.

Floods can hurt people and damage their homes. But Mississippi floods also do some good. They leave **fertile** soil on fields. Fertile soil is land that is good for growing crops.

Trees, vines, and flowers grow on the wet land of a swamp.

Barges carry goods on the Mississippi River.

Name _____ Date _____

Chapter Checkup

▶ Darken the circle by the answer that best completes each sentence.

1. A gulf is like
   - Ⓐ a bay.
   - Ⓑ a river.
   - Ⓒ a lake.
   - Ⓓ an ocean.

2. Some hurricanes begin over the Gulf of Mexico or over the
   - Ⓐ Mississippi River.
   - Ⓑ Southeast.
   - Ⓒ Northeast.
   - Ⓓ Atlantic Ocean.

3. The Coastal Plain is flat and has lots of
   - Ⓐ mountains.
   - Ⓑ hurricanes.
   - Ⓒ good soil.
   - Ⓓ snow.

4. A swamp is
   - Ⓐ dry.
   - Ⓑ wet.
   - Ⓒ snowy.
   - Ⓓ very hot.

5. The second-longest river in the United States is the
   - Ⓐ Everglades.
   - Ⓑ Savannah.
   - Ⓒ Mississippi.
   - Ⓓ Ohio.

6. Water that rises and covers the land is a
   - Ⓐ hurricane.
   - Ⓑ gulf.
   - Ⓒ swamp.
   - Ⓓ flood.

THINKING AND WRITING

Why is the Mississippi River a resource for the Southeast Region? Give reasons for your answer.

_____
_____
_____
_____
_____

Name _____ Date _____

Chapter 7: People of the Southeast Region

What is it like to live in the Southeast Region? Let's find out! First, we'll visit the region over 200 years ago.

Long Ago: Old Virginia in 1774

It's two o'clock and time for lunch. The King's Arms Tavern in Williamsburg, Virginia, is filled with people today.

The government of the colony meets here. Representatives from Virginia come to Williamsburg, the capital, to discuss laws.

▶ **Today, Williamsburg is not the capital of Virginia. Look at the map on page 39 and find the capital of Virginia. Write the name here.**

_____

King's Arms Tavern

Name _____ Date _____

The first governor wanted Williamsburg to become a big city. He made the streets straight, not like the curving streets in country towns. The main street of this city is 100 feet wide! Williamsburg has a school, but not everyone can go there. Most children have to help their parents in their shops. Slaves are not allowed to go to school. But there is a school for American Indians who want to learn to read and write English.

Blacksmith

Williamsburg has many stores. Do you need a new pair of shoes? You can't just walk into a shoe store and buy them. First, the shoemaker has to measure your feet. Then, he'll make shoes to fit you. You can come back in a week to pick them up.

There are many businesses here in Williamsburg. There's a blacksmith who works with iron and steel. He makes shoes for horses and fixes tools. And there are shops where barrels or baskets or wigs are made. People in Williamsburg wear wigs whenever they get dressed up.

That's how it was in 1774. If you visit Williamsburg today, you'll have a surprise. It never became a big city. In fact, it still looks the same! The King's Arms still serves meals, and people still make baskets by hand. That is because the city is a "living museum" where we can go to see how Americans lived here more than 200 years ago.

➤ **Write the name of a building in your town that you think should always be kept the way it is now. Tell why. Write your answer here.**

_____
_____
_____
_____
_____
_____

Many people enjoy the sun and sand at Miami Beach, Florida.

Who Lives in the Southeast Today?

Over 70 million people live in the Southeast. More than 60 million live in the Northeast. But the Southeast is not as crowded.

➤ **Compare the maps on page 25 and page 39. Which region has more land? Write your answer here.**

_____

Every year, more people move to the Southeast. Some people come to find jobs. Others come because they like warm weather. The lower part of the region is called the **Sunbelt** because it has a sunny climate.

People have moved to the Southeast from many parts of the world. From the 1600s to the early 1900s, many people came from Europe. Since the 1960s, thousands of people from Cuba have moved to Florida. People from China, the Philippines, and Vietnam have come to the region, too. Almost half of all African Americans in the United States live in the Southeast.

Where Do People Live in the Region?

In the Southeast, more people live in small towns than in cities. But there are large cities in each state of the region. New Orleans, Louisiana, is the busiest port city in the United States. It is on the Mississippi River.

Products and crops from many states are shipped to New Orleans on the river. At New Orleans, they are put on bigger ships. From the Mississippi River, the ships move out into the Gulf of Mexico. From the Gulf of Mexico, they can go around the world.

➤ **Look at the map on page 41. Ships leave the Gulf of Mexico to take products to other countries. If they go east, on what ocean will they travel?**

_____

New Orleans was once a colony of France. Later, France sold New Orleans to the United States. Some of the buildings in New Orleans look like old buildings in France. Other parts look very modern. In 2005, much of New Orleans was flooded by hurricane Katrina. The city is slowly recovering from great destruction.

Many tourists like to visit the French Quarter in New Orleans.

Atlanta, Georgia

Atlanta, Georgia, is one of the biggest cities in the Southeast. Atlanta was a small city until about 100 years ago. Everything changed when the railroads reached the city. First, the railroad companies built the rail lines along the Coastal Plain.

➤ **Why would railroad companies first build lines on the plain? Write your answer here.**

_____

_____

_____

Then, other railroads were built from the coast to the mountains. Atlanta was at the place where all the railroads met. So Atlanta became a good place to have a business. You could ship products from Atlanta all over the United States. Today, Atlanta is one of the most important U.S. cities for business. The 1996 Summer Olympic Games were held in Atlanta.

Miami, Florida, is very warm in the winter. People from the north like to take vacations there. Tourism is an important business in Florida all year long.

Working in the Southeast Region

The most important resource in the Southeast has always been fertile land. In the 1800s, cotton was the most important crop in the Southeast. People grew cotton on large farms called **plantations** and sold it to countries all over the world.

Name _____   Date _____

Cotton is still an important crop because we use it to make clothing. Factories in North Carolina make more cloth than factories in any other state in the United States. The flowchart on this page shows how cotton from the Southeast is used to make jeans.

➤ Write <u>SEW</u> on the picture that shows how pieces of cloth are put together with a sewing machine.

Write <u>SHIP</u> on the picture that shows how the jeans get to the stores.

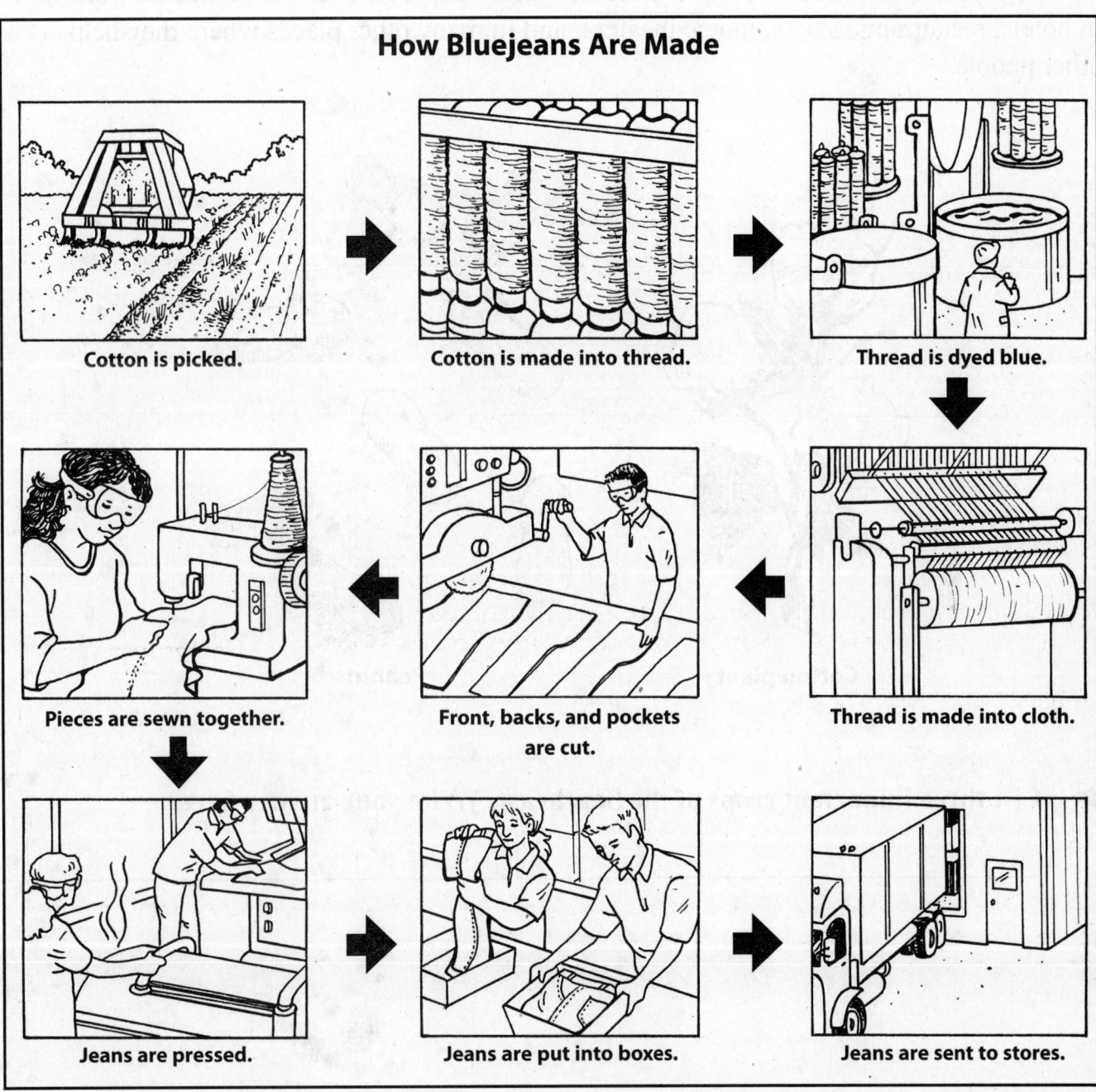

The warm climate of the Southeast is good for growing certain crops. Most of the oranges grown in the United States come from Florida. Rice is another crop grown in the Southeast. Another important crop of the Southeast is peanuts. Did you know that peanut soup and peanut pie are popular foods in parts of the Southeast?

One city in the Southeast is known for a very different kind of product. Nashville, Tennessee, is called the capital of country music. Stars of country music make records there. The music business is one of the biggest businesses in the city.

Many people in the Southeast have service jobs. People all over the Southeast work in hotels, restaurants, stores, movie theaters, and in many other places where they help other people.

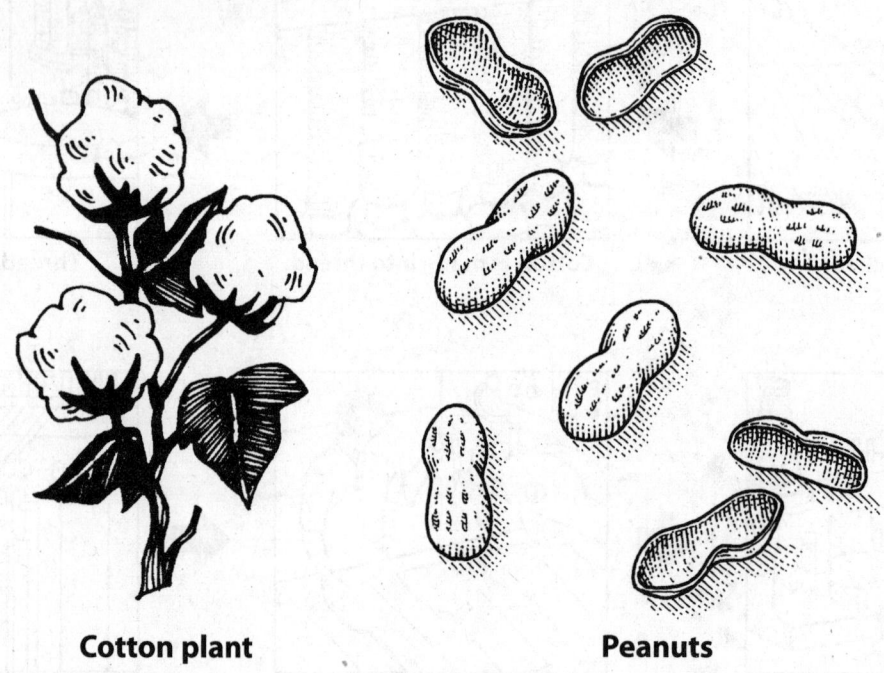

Cotton plant   **Peanuts**

▶ **List three important crops of the Southeast. Write your answer here.**

_____

Name _____ Date _____

Chapter Checkup

▶ **Darken the circle by the answer that best completes each sentence.**

1. The city that still looks the way it did about 200 years ago is
   - Ⓐ Atlanta.
   - Ⓑ New Orleans.
   - Ⓒ Miami.
   - Ⓓ Williamsburg.

2. The Mississippi River is important to the city of New Orleans because
   - Ⓐ the city needs a lot of water.
   - Ⓑ ships carry products on it.
   - Ⓒ farmers like to swim in the river.
   - Ⓓ it is next to Atlanta, Georgia.

3. The busiest port city in the United States is
   - Ⓐ New Orleans.
   - Ⓑ Miami.
   - Ⓒ Atlanta.
   - Ⓓ Williamsburg.

4. Atlanta became a big city after
   - Ⓐ the French Quarter was built.
   - Ⓑ the farmers left.
   - Ⓒ railroads reached the city.
   - Ⓓ plantations were started.

5. Long ago, the biggest crop in the Southeast was
   - Ⓐ cotton.
   - Ⓑ peanuts.
   - Ⓒ oranges.
   - Ⓓ rice.

6. The city of Nashville is known for its
   - Ⓐ buildings.
   - Ⓑ music.
   - Ⓒ railroads.
   - Ⓓ jeans.

THINKING AND WRITING

Name a place you would like to visit that still looks the way it did 200 years ago. Give your reasons.

_____
_____
_____
_____

Name _____ Date _____

Unit 3 Skill Builder: Reading a Table

You have read about some famous places in the Southeast Region. The table below tells you about more interesting places. Maybe you've already heard of some of them!

Famous Places in the Southeast Region		
Place	**Location**	**Description**
Mammoth Cave	Kentucky	Unusual cave containing lakes, rivers, and waterfalls
Okefenokee Swamp	Georgia	Large swamp that is home to raccoons, opossums, alligators, bobcats, and many types of birds and plants
Walt Disney World	Florida	Huge amusement park visited by millions of people from around the world

▶ **Use the table to answer these questions.**

1. What state would you be in if you were visiting Okefenokee Swamp?

   _____

2. If you visited Kentucky, what famous place could you visit?

   _____

3. Which famous place would you visit if you wanted to see interesting animals?

   _____

4. Which place was built by people?

   _____

Unit 3 Activity: Working a Puzzle

➤ Each sentence below has a word missing. Write the missing word in the correct location in the puzzle.

ACROSS

2. A place where the land is always wet is called a _____.

4. A large body of water that joins an ocean and is partly surrounded by land is a _____.

6. The _____ River is wide enough for big ships.

8. The Southeast once had large farms called _____.

DOWN

1. A storm with strong winds and heavy rain is a _____.

3. The King's _____ was a tavern in Williamsburg.

5. New Orleans was once part of a colony belonging to _____.

7. Two important crops of the Southeast are cotton and _____.

Name _____   Date _____

Unit 3 Test

▶ **Darken the circle by the answer that best completes each sentence.**

1. The southern part of the Southeast Region is along the
   - Ⓐ Atlantic Ocean.
   - Ⓑ Gulf of Mexico.
   - Ⓒ Pacific Ocean.
   - Ⓓ Appalachian Mountains.

2. A large body of water partly surrounded by land is called a
   - Ⓐ lake.
   - Ⓑ port.
   - Ⓒ river.
   - Ⓓ gulf.

3. The Southeast sometimes has storms with strong winds and heavy rain called
   - Ⓐ gulfs.
   - Ⓑ swamps.
   - Ⓒ hurricanes.
   - Ⓓ floods.

4. The Mississippi River flows into the
   - Ⓐ Atlantic Ocean.
   - Ⓑ Pacific Ocean.
   - Ⓒ Everglades.
   - Ⓓ Gulf of Mexico.

5. Soil that is good for growing crops is
   - Ⓐ fertile.
   - Ⓑ muddy.
   - Ⓒ swampy.
   - Ⓓ in the mountains.

6. Two cities in the Southeast are
   - Ⓐ New Orleans and Atlanta.
   - Ⓑ New York and Chicago.
   - Ⓒ Philadelphia and Boston.
   - Ⓓ Baltimore and Cleveland.

7. The busiest port city in the United States is
   - Ⓐ Nashville.
   - Ⓑ New Orleans.
   - Ⓒ Miami.
   - Ⓓ Atlanta.

8. Two of the Southeast's important crops are
   - Ⓐ wheat and corn.
   - Ⓑ soybeans and rye.
   - Ⓒ peas and carrots.
   - Ⓓ rice and cotton.

THINKING AND WRITING

Why is the Mississippi River important to farming and manufacturing in the Southeast?

_____

Name _____ Date _____

Chapter 8: Geography of the North Central Region

Like the Southeast Region, the North Central Region has 12 states. But the North Central Region is much flatter than the Southeast. There are few mountains and hills.

States, Cities, and Transportation

➤ Suppose you have to drive to the 12 state capitals in the region. You can go into each state only once. Start in Columbus, Ohio. Use a pencil to draw lines to connect the 12 capitals on the map below.

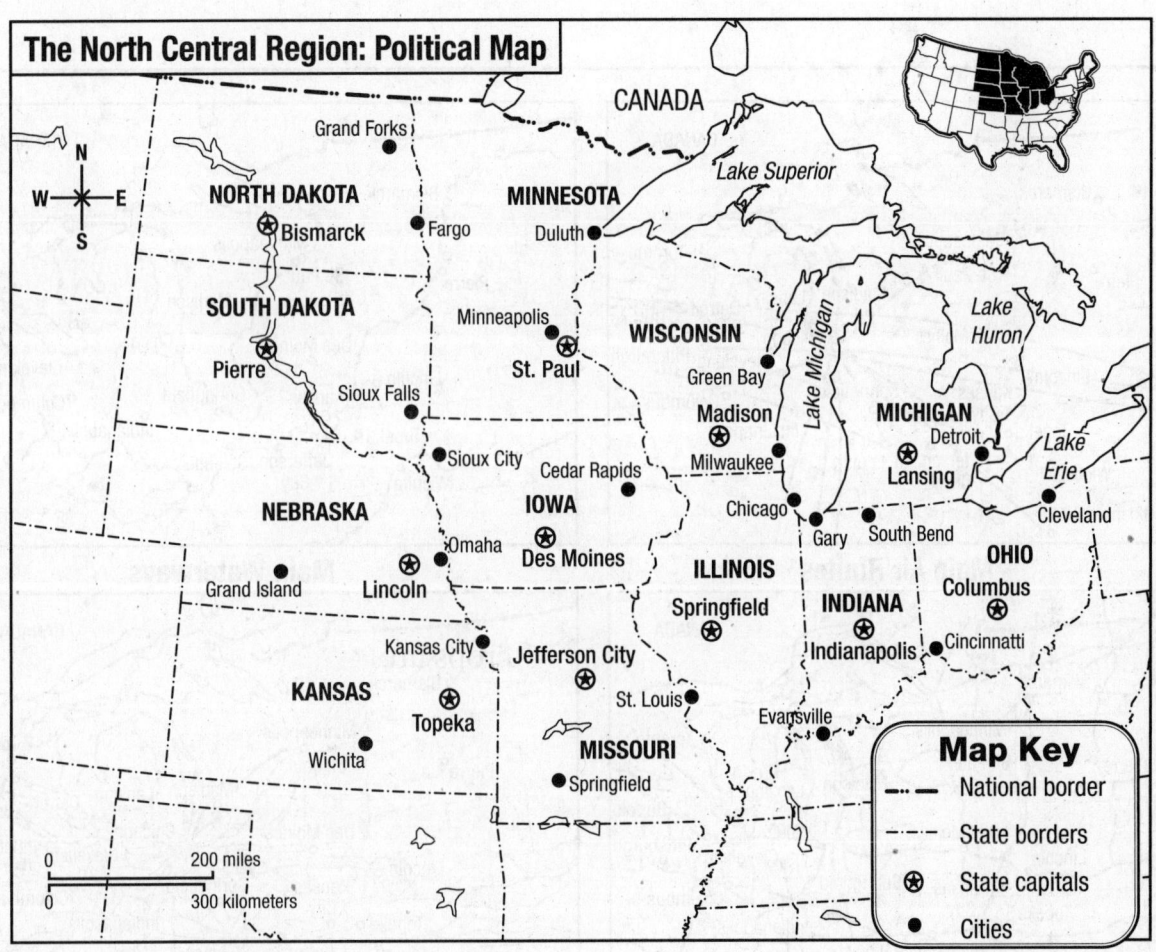

Name _____ Date _____

The lines you drew on page 55 show a **route** of travel. A route is the way to go someplace. Look at the four maps on this page. Each map shows a different kind of transportation route. Airplanes fly between cities. Ships go on lakes and rivers. Cars and trucks drive on highways. Trains travel on railroads.

▶ **Look at the map called Main Air Routes. Each solid line shows an airplane route. Which city has the most airplanes flying in and out of it? Write your answer here.**

_____

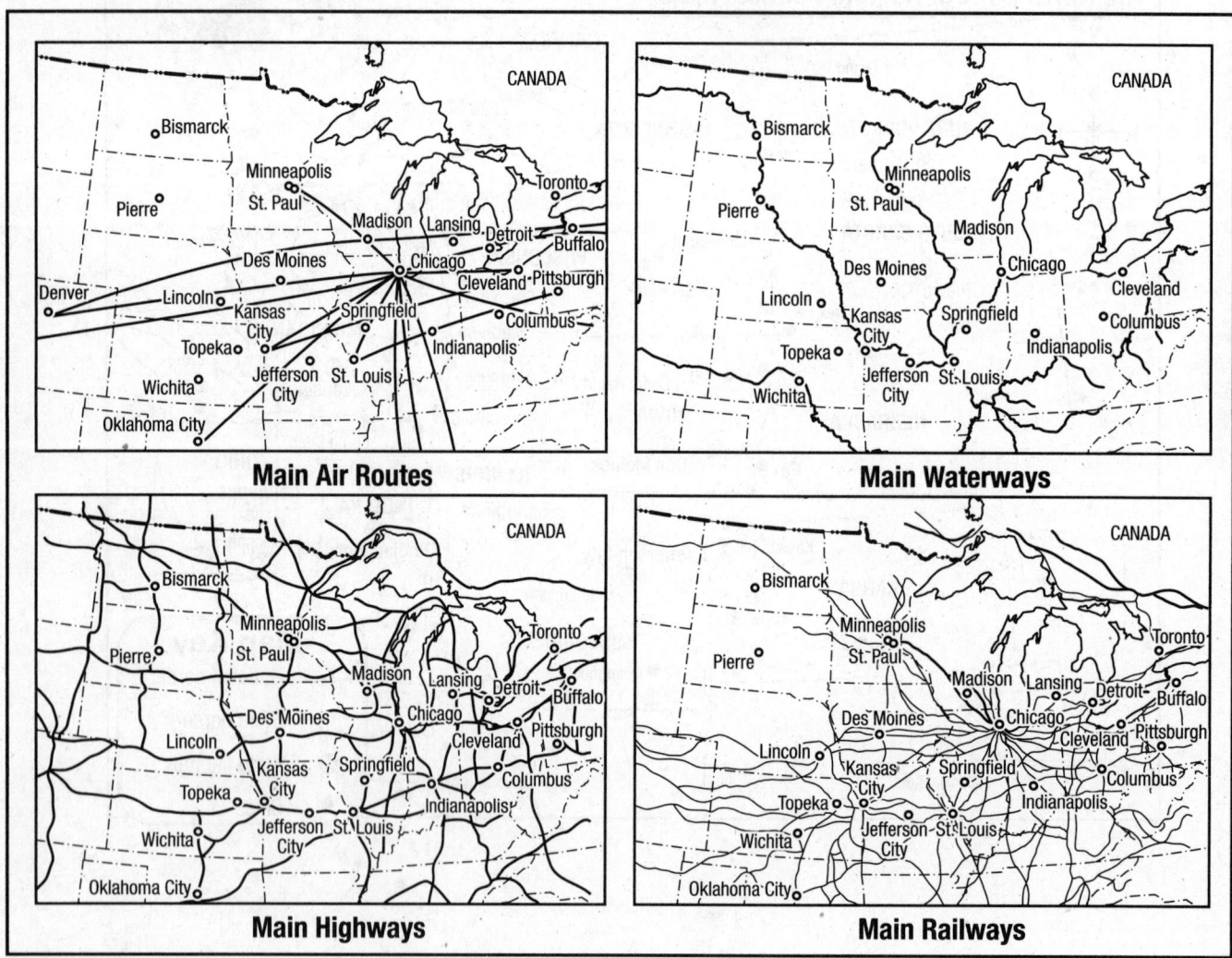

56

© Houghton Mifflin Harcourt Publishing Company

Unit 4, Chapter 8
Core Skills Social Studies, Grade 4

Name _____   Date _____

The Land and the Great Lakes

When you studied physical maps of other regions, you learned that the key shows the shading that stands for different landforms.

▶ **Look at the map and the key. Write the name of the landform that makes up most of the North Central Region.**

Prairie

_____

▶ **Look at the west side of the map. Circle the words *Great Plains* and *Central Plains*.**

The Central Plains are very flat. They were once covered with grass. In some places, the grass was nine feet tall! These great areas of grass were called **prairies**. Today, farmers grow wheat and corn on the prairies.

The Great Plains are not as flat as the Central Plains. It doesn't rain as much there, either. Instead of farming, people raise cattle.

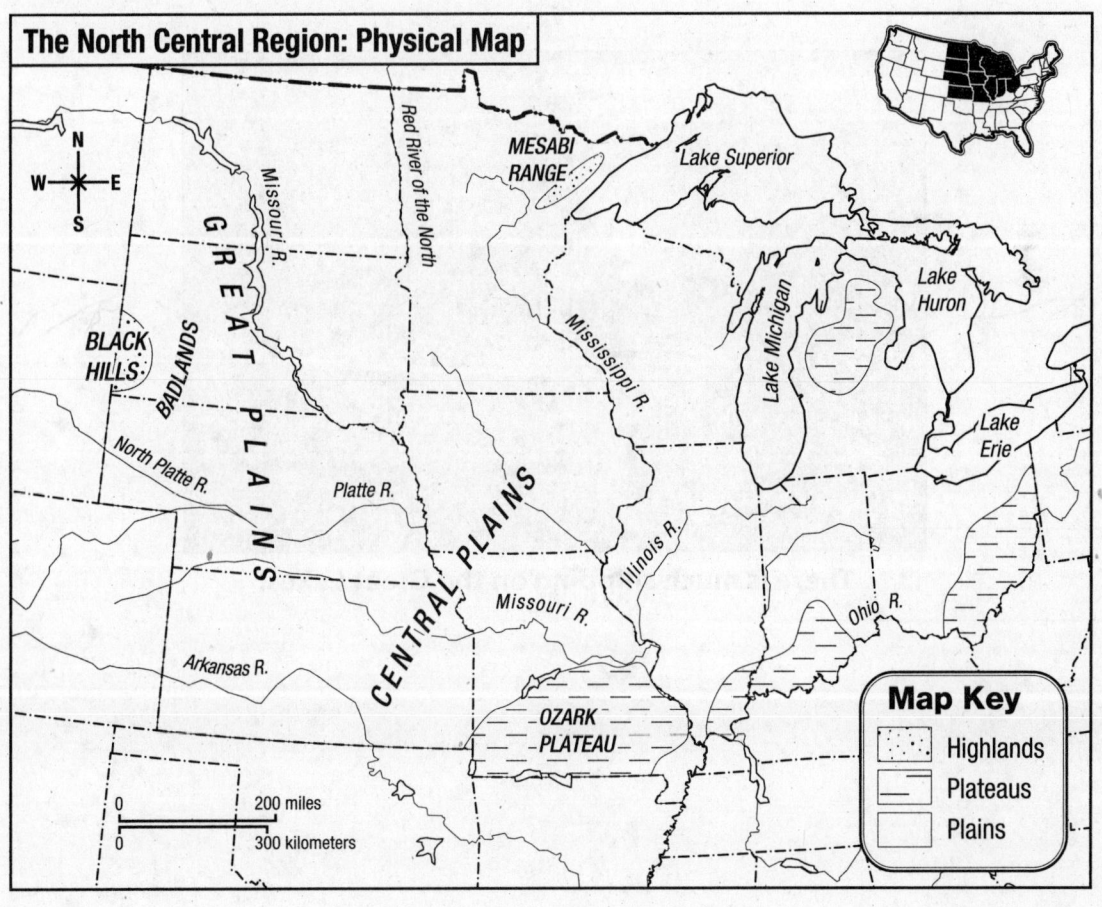

© Houghton Mifflin Harcourt Publishing Company

57

Unit 4, Chapter 8
Core Skills Social Studies, Grade 4

Name _____ Date _____

The North Central Region has lakes and rivers that ships can travel on. Some cities in the North Central Region are important ports.

➤ **Find the four biggest lakes on the map on page 57. Write their names here.**

_____

_____

We call these large lakes the Great Lakes. There is a fifth Great Lake, called Lake Ontario. It is in the Northeast Region. You can see Lake Ontario on the map on page 27.

Turn back to page 56. Look at the Main Waterways map. You can see that short rivers connect the Great Lakes. Longer rivers connect these lakes to cities and other rivers.

Look at the map on page 57. Find the dotted line that leads from Lake Michigan to the Illinois River. The dotted line is a **canal**. A canal is a waterway built by people. Canals link bodies of water so ships can travel from one waterway to another.

➤ **On the map on page 57, trace with a pencil the route a ship would take from Lake Michigan to the Mississippi River.**

There is much shipping on the Great Lakes.

Name _____ Date _____

Chapter Checkup

➤ **Darken the circle by the answer that best completes each sentence.**

1. What is most of the land like in the North Central Region?
   - Ⓐ hilly
   - Ⓑ mostly rivers
   - Ⓒ flat
   - Ⓓ mostly plateaus

2. Which city has a very busy airport?
   - Ⓐ Duluth
   - Ⓑ Kansas City
   - Ⓒ St. Louis
   - Ⓓ Chicago

3. The two areas of plains in the North Central Region are the Great Plains and the
   - Ⓐ Prairie Plains.
   - Ⓑ Central Plains.
   - Ⓒ Middle Plains.
   - Ⓓ Northern Plains.

4. What is a prairie?
   - Ⓐ a small mountain
   - Ⓑ a great area of grass
   - Ⓒ a large farm
   - Ⓓ a lake

5. A waterway built by people is a
   - Ⓐ canal.
   - Ⓑ route.
   - Ⓒ harbor.
   - Ⓓ Great Lake.

6. Which of these is not a Great Lake?
   - Ⓐ Superior
   - Ⓑ Huron
   - Ⓒ Minnesota
   - Ⓓ Erie

THINKING AND WRITING

Airplanes travel faster than cars. Why might someone want to drive instead of fly?

_____
_____
_____
_____
_____

Name _____

Chapter 9: People of the North Central Region

The pioneers headed west in covered wagons.

Many people went to the plains of the North Central Region in the 1800s. They were **pioneers**—people who go to live in a new place. Let's read a letter written in 1886 from Molly to her cousin Barbara. Molly writes about the trip her pioneer family took to the Great Plains.

Long Ago: The Treeless Plains

September 2, 1886

Dear Cousin Barbara,

You wanted to know how we are getting along since leaving Indiana. Well, I will tell you.

Two years ago, my mother and father decided to go to Nebraska, where there was a lot of free land. The government said anyone who would build a farm could have the land. This is called <u>homesteading</u>. My parents thought that sounded like a pretty good deal.

We left Indiana in a covered wagon. There is a railroad to Omaha, Nebraska, but tickets cost a lot of money. And my parents had to take along all their farm tools. We knew there weren't many stores in Nebraska.

➤ Write the names of some things you think Molly's pioneer family needed.

_____

_____

_____

Name _____ Date _____

We were very happy when we left for Nebraska. We sang songs all the way to the Mississippi River. There we met a man who said, "You're headed for the Great American Desert? Well, good luck, you'll need it."

He didn't mean the kind of desert that's full of sand. He meant that the land was flat and empty. Here in Nebraska there are no trees at all, just tall grass. And there aren't many rivers.

▶ **What landform is Molly talking about? Write your answer here.**

_____

When we reached our land in Nebraska, Father grabbed a shovel and started digging. "Look at this color," Father said. "This is the richest dirt I've ever seen. It will be easy to grow crops here."

Since there are no trees, my parents could not build the usual kind of house. Instead, they made one out of <u>sod</u>. Sod is blocks of dirt with grass growing in it. The roots of the grass hold the dirt together. My parents piled the blocks of sod on top of one another. Finally, we got our one-room sod house built.

It is dark inside our sod house. But it stays cool in the hot summers and warm in the cold winters.

I hope you and your family are well. Telling you about our life here in Nebraska has been fun. I hope you'll write again soon.

Love,
Cousin Molly

The pioneers plowed fields and made butter.

▶ **Look at the picture on this page. The pioneers are plowing fields and making butter. How do people do these things today? Write your answer here.**

_____

_____

Name _____   Date _____

How Many People Live in the Region Today?

Over 70 million people live in the 12 states of the North Central Region. But more than half of these people live in just three states: Illinois, Ohio, and Michigan.

Why don't more people live in the other nine states? The main reason is that the nine states are where the farms are. Farms need lots of space.

Population is the number of people who live in a place. A population map gives you an idea of how many people live in an area. It also shows you where people live.

Find Nebraska on the map below. The dots and lines show where people live in that state. Notice that the dots are very far apart in some areas of the state. Those are farm areas. Now look at Ohio. The areas with many dots are near cities.

▶ **Which part of South Dakota has the most people?**

_____

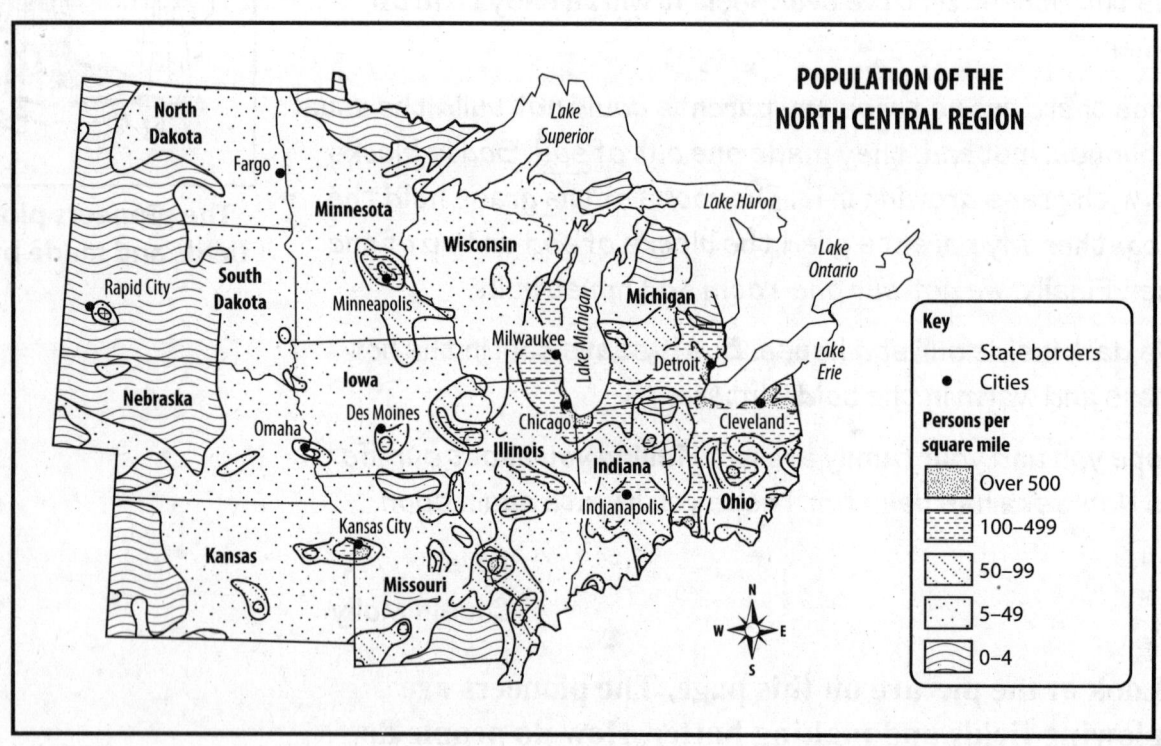

Name _____ Date _____

Where Do People Live in the Region?

You know that most people in the region live in Illinois, Ohio, and Michigan. All of these states are near the Great Lakes. Many of the large cities of the region are ports on the Great Lakes. These cities have many factories and businesses. Let's take a look at some of these cities.

Chicago, Illinois, is the largest city in the region. It is the third-largest city in the United States. Almost three million people live there. Since the 1960s many immigrants from Mexico and Asia have moved to Chicago.

▶ **Find Chicago on the map on page 55. What Great Lake is it next to? Write your answer here.**

_____

Chicago is a major transportation center. It is a major port. O'Hare Airport in Chicago is one of the largest and busiest airports in the world. Chicago is also a major center for railroad transportation.

The Sears Tower is the tallest building in Chicago, Illinois.

Name _____ Date _____

More than 80,000 people live in Duluth, Minnesota. Duluth is an important port city. Products such as iron ore and grain are sent from Duluth to other places in huge ships. Some ships are as long as four city blocks!

➤ **One place the iron ore is shipped to is Gary, Indiana. Find Duluth and Gary on the map on page 55. What lakes would a ship travel across to get from Duluth to Gary? Draw the route you would follow on the map on page 55.**

St. Louis, Missouri, is a port on the Mississippi River. It began as a French colony. American Indians and other people took furs there to sell. People traveling west found it easy to get to St. Louis. Soon the city became a major port and a railroad center.

Today, all kinds of products are shipped from St. Louis. It is a bigger port than Chicago.

So many pioneers passed through St. Louis that it was called "the gateway to the West." The Gateway Arch celebrates that name.

Name _____   Date _____

Working in the North Central Region

Service businesses are very important in the North Central Region. Other businesses are also important to the region. Near the Great Lakes, people manufacture a lot of things. On the plains, people have farms and ranches.

Many American cars are made near the Great Lakes. Detroit, Michigan, is the center of the United States automobile business. In 1903, Henry Ford began making cars in Detroit. His "Model T" was the first automobile that many people could buy.

The Model T was made on an **assembly line**. Each worker does one job over and over again on the cars on the assembly line.

➤ **Would you like to work on an assembly line? Why? Write your answer here.**

_____

_____

Cars are still built on an assembly line.

One of the reasons Henry Ford decided to build his factory in Detroit was that it is a port. Detroit is on a river between Lake Huron and Lake Erie. Ships carrying steel and other things used to build cars arrive in Detroit every day. Other ships carry finished cars from Detroit to other cities and to countries around the world.

Ships also travel across the Great Lakes carrying grains such as corn and wheat and other foods. Corn is the biggest crop grown in the North Central Region. Corn farmers of the region grow more corn than any other farmers in the world.

A lot of the grain grown in the region is fed to cattle and other animals. That's because there are many farms in the North Central Region that just raise animals.

➤ **What kind of land do a lot of ranchers use to raise animals in the region?**

_____

Dairy cattle are raised in every state of the region. We get milk, cheese, and other foods from dairy cattle. Part of your breakfast this morning may have come from a cow in Iowa!

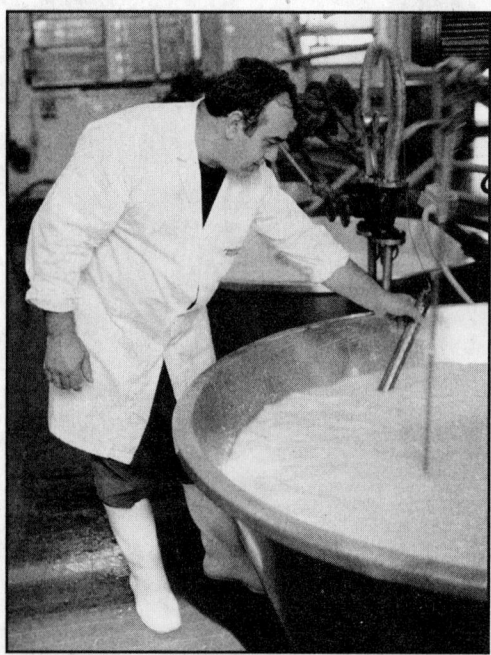

The North Central Region is famous for its cheese and other dairy products. Here a worker tests some cheese.

Name _____ Date _____

Chapter Checkup

▶ Darken the circle by the answer that best completes each sentence.

1. Under the homesteading plan, the government offered people moving to the Great Plains
   - Ⓐ a covered wagon.
   - Ⓑ land for farming.
   - Ⓒ five hundred dollars.
   - Ⓓ a brick house.

2. A sod house is made of
   - Ⓐ bricks.
   - Ⓑ wood.
   - Ⓒ rocks.
   - Ⓓ dirt.

3. The biggest cities in the North Central Region are near
   - Ⓐ lakes.
   - Ⓑ plateaus.
   - Ⓒ mountains.
   - Ⓓ oceans.

4. The city with the most people in the North Central Region is
   - Ⓐ Chicago, Illinois.
   - Ⓑ Detroit, Michigan.
   - Ⓒ St. Louis, Missouri.
   - Ⓓ Duluth, Minnesota.

5. The center of the American automobile business is
   - Ⓐ Duluth, Minnesota.
   - Ⓑ Chicago, Illinois.
   - Ⓒ Detroit, Michigan.
   - Ⓓ St. Louis, Missouri.

6. The biggest crop in the North Central Region is
   - Ⓐ cattle.
   - Ⓑ sugar.
   - Ⓒ milk.
   - Ⓓ corn.

THINKING AND WRITING

Write a menu for a meal that has at least two food items made from corn.

_____

_____

_____

_____

Name _____   Date _____

Unit 4 Skill Builder: Planning Routes

In this unit you learned that ships carry products from one Great Lakes port to another. But did you know that ships can travel from the Great Lakes all the way to the Atlantic Ocean? In the 1800s, people built canals to connect the Great Lakes to the St. Lawrence River, which flows into the Atlantic Ocean. Look at the map below.

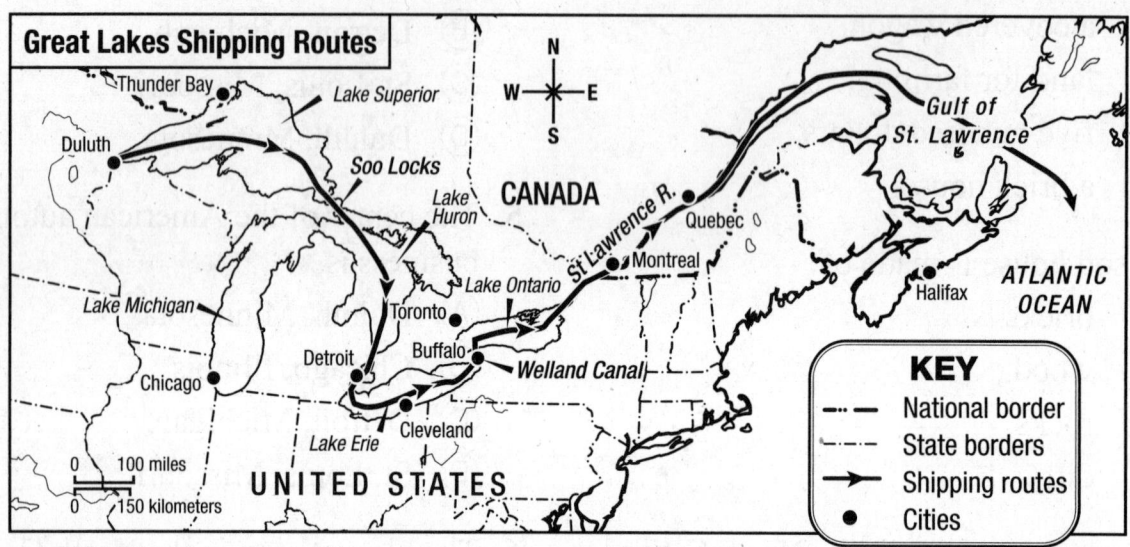

1. Which Great Lake is connected to the St. Lawrence River?

_____

2. Draw the route a ship would take to carry automobiles from Detroit, Michigan, to the port at Halifax, Nova Scotia.

3. Factories in Battle Creek, Michigan, need grain to make breakfast cereals. Ships carrying grain leave from Thunder Bay in Ontario, Canada. With your finger, trace a route from Thunder Bay to Detroit, Michigan. On which two Great Lakes will the ships travel?

_____

Name _____ Date _____

Unit 4 Test

▶ **Darken the circle by the answer that best completes each sentence.**

1. The North Central Region has few
   - Ⓐ rivers and lakes.
   - Ⓑ large cities.
   - Ⓒ high mountains.
   - Ⓓ farms and factories.

2. A way to travel from one place to another is called a
   - Ⓐ route.
   - Ⓑ map.
   - Ⓒ distance scale.
   - Ⓓ prairie.

3. The five Great Lakes are Superior, Erie, Michigan, Huron, and
   - Ⓐ Illinois.
   - Ⓑ Atlantic.
   - Ⓒ Mississippi.
   - Ⓓ Ontario.

4. In the 1800s, the government gave land to people who agreed to build farms. These people were
   - Ⓐ Nebraskans.
   - Ⓑ American Indians.
   - Ⓒ homesteaders.
   - Ⓓ ranchers.

5. One way to connect two bodies of water is to build a
   - Ⓐ lake.
   - Ⓑ river.
   - Ⓒ harbor.
   - Ⓓ canal.

6. A map that shows about how many people live in an area is a
   - Ⓐ climate map.
   - Ⓑ population map.
   - Ⓒ weather map.
   - Ⓓ physical map.

7. Duluth, St. Louis, Detroit, and Chicago are
   - Ⓐ farming centers.
   - Ⓑ Great Lakes.
   - Ⓒ port cities.
   - Ⓓ capital cities.

8. Farmers in the North Central Region grow
   - Ⓐ rice and cotton.
   - Ⓑ wheat and corn.
   - Ⓒ prairie grasses.
   - Ⓓ sod.

THINKING AND WRITING

How would you choose to travel from Duluth to St. Louis—by car, by airplane, or by boat? Explain your answer.

Name _____ Date _____

Chapter 10: Geography of the Rocky Mountain Region

Where do you think the Rocky Mountain Region got its name? If you said from one of the region's major landforms, you're right. In this chapter, you'll find out about them.

Rocky Mountain States

➤ **Look at the map. The capital cities are far apart. Use the distance scale to measure the distance in miles between Helena, Montana, and Salt Lake City, Utah. Write the distance here.**

_____

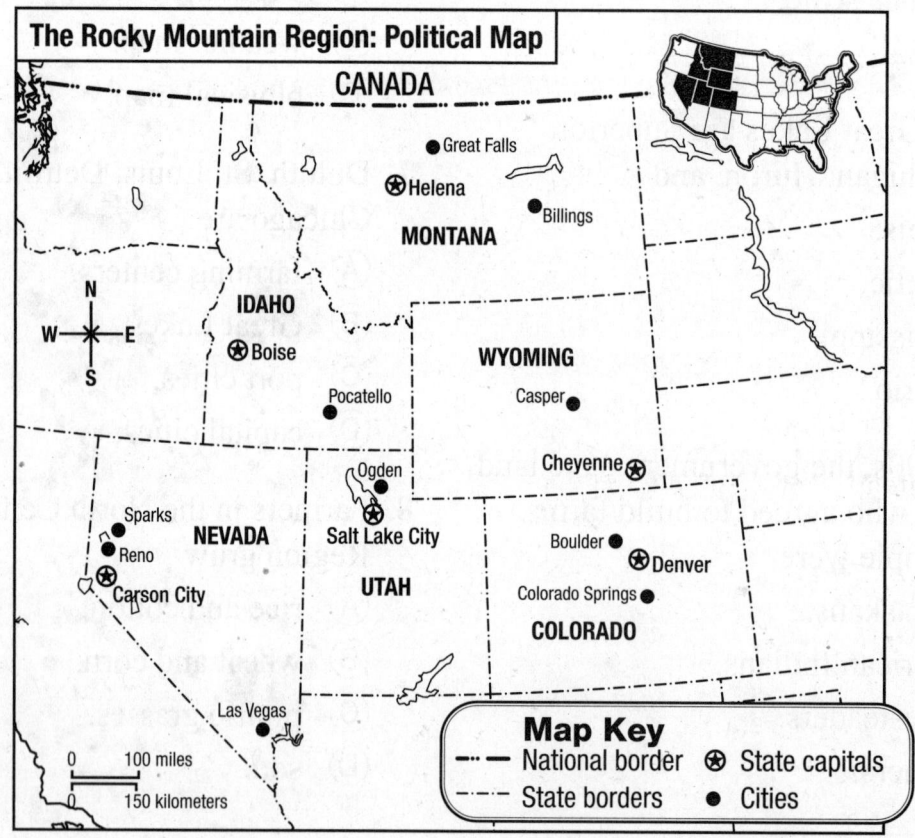

Name _____ Date _____

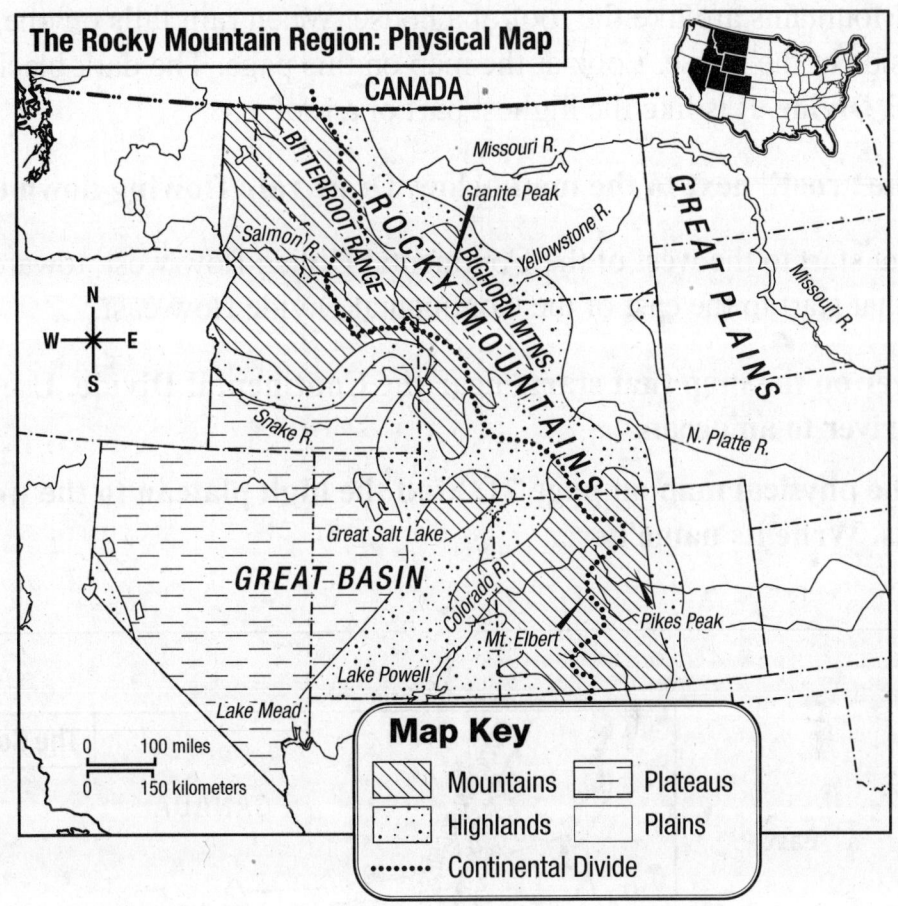

Mountains, Canyons, and Basins

The Rocky Mountains run through five of the six states of this region. The other state is on a high plateau. In Chapter 1 you learned that a plateau is a high, flat area of land.

▶ **Look at the map key on this page. Find the shading for plateaus. Which state is mostly a plateau? Write your answer here.**

_____

The Rocky Mountains are part of a long chain of mountains. This chain reaches from Alaska to the bottom of South America at the Andes Mountains. Look at the map on page 72. You can see where part of the Rocky Mountains stretches down from Canada and across the United States.

Name _____ Date _____

The Rocky Mountains are like the roof of a house. When rain falls on one side of a roof, it rolls off that side of the house. Look at the map on this page. The dark black line shows the **Continental Divide**. It is like the highest part of a roof.

➤ **Look at the "roof" next to the map below. Draw rain flowing down each side.**

All rivers that start to the west of the Continental Divide flow west, toward the Pacific Ocean. Rivers that start to the east of the Continental Divide flow east.

➤ **Find a river on the map that starts near the Continental Divide. Use a pencil to trace the river to an ocean.**

Look at the physical map on page 71. Find the high plateau to the west of the mountains. Write its name here.

_____

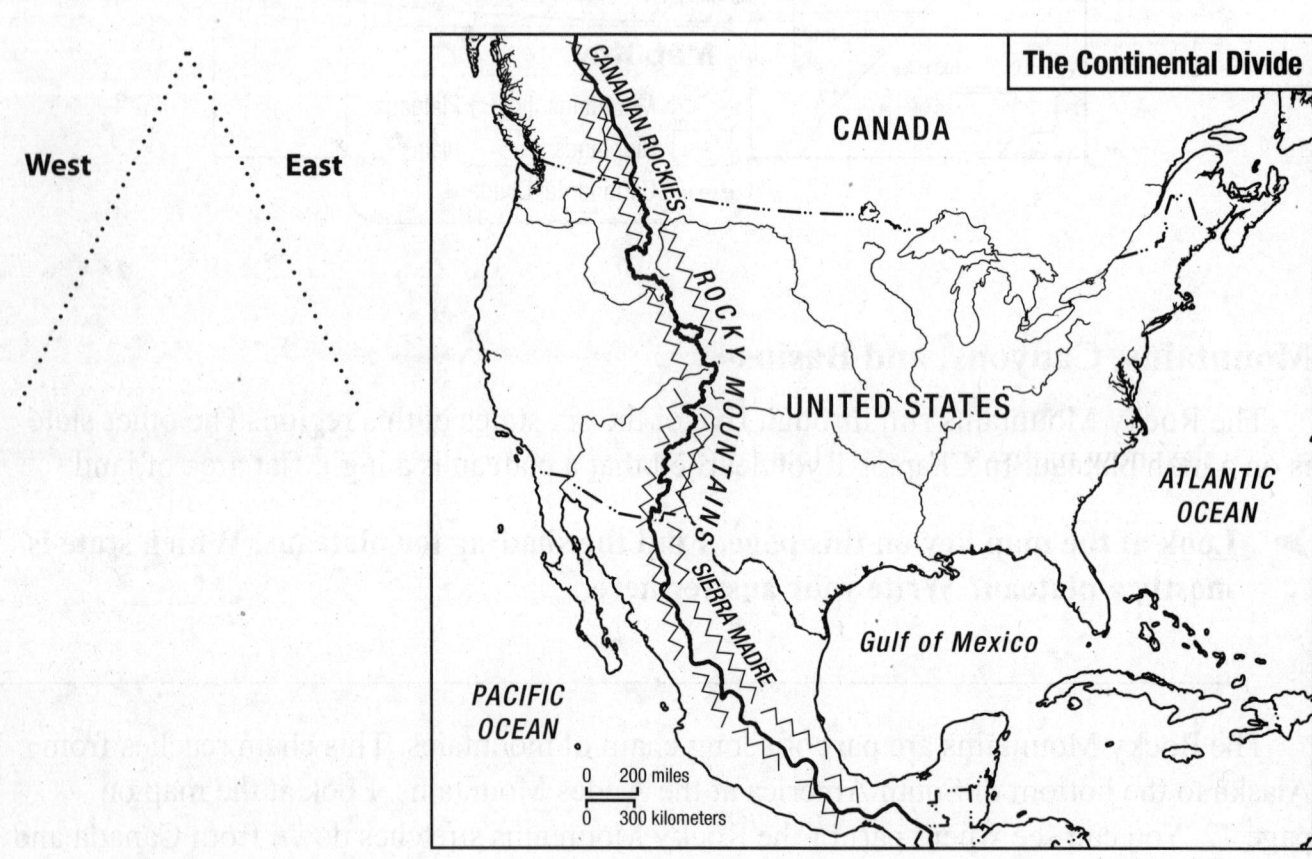

Glaciers move at a rate of a few inches per day. As they move, they help to shape the land.

A **basin** is a landform shaped like a giant bowl. It has high sides all around. Once, the Great Basin was filled with water. There was a huge lake there. Over thousands of years, most of the water dried up. The water that is left now is so full of minerals, especially salt, that it is called the Great Salt Lake. Find the Great Salt Lake on the map on page 71.

It doesn't rain much in the Great Basin. Most of the water comes from ice and snow far up in the Rocky Mountains. Huge fields of ice and snow called **glaciers** lie on the highest slopes. Even in summer, the mountains are covered with snow.

As the snow melts, the water flows into rivers. The rushing waters pull away dirt and rocks, forming **canyons**. Canyons are deep, narrow valleys formed after hundreds of thousands of years.

➤ **Look at the photograph on the right. What natural resource made the canyon? Write your answer here.**

_____

Moving water in rivers can carve away rock to form canyons.

Name _____ Date _____

Chapter Checkup

▶ **Darken the circle by the answer that best completes each sentence.**

1. The Rocky Mountains run through all the states in the region except
   - Ⓐ Wyoming.
   - Ⓑ Idaho.
   - Ⓒ Nevada.
   - Ⓓ Colorado.

2. The Rocky Mountain chain stretches down from Alaska all the way through to the bottom of
   - Ⓐ Colorado.
   - Ⓑ South America.
   - Ⓒ Canada.
   - Ⓓ Nevada.

3. Rivers that are west of the Continental Divide flow toward the
   - Ⓐ Atlantic Ocean.
   - Ⓑ Pacific Ocean.
   - Ⓒ Great Basin.
   - Ⓓ Great Lakes.

4. A basin is a landform that is shaped like a giant
   - Ⓐ football.
   - Ⓑ castle.
   - Ⓒ bowl.
   - Ⓓ canyon.

5. The Great Salt Lake is located in
   - Ⓐ the Great Basin.
   - Ⓑ the Rocky Mountains.
   - Ⓒ the state of Colorado.
   - Ⓓ the Continental Divide.

6. Deep, narrow valleys are called
   - Ⓐ canyons.
   - Ⓑ basins.
   - Ⓒ mountains.
   - Ⓓ plains.

THINKING AND WRITING

Find Sparks, Nevada, on the map on page 70. Use what you learned in this chapter to describe what it might be like to live there.

_____
_____
_____
_____

Chapter 11: People of the Rocky Mountain Region

In this chapter you'll find out how people in the Rocky Mountain Region live today. But first let's meet one group who learned how to live in the region more than 150 years ago.

Long Ago in the Rockies: The Mountain Men

Jed Smith was born in New York State in 1799. As a boy, he learned how to live in the woods. At the age of 22, Jed headed west in search of adventure. He joined a group of explorers.

➤ **What do you think Jed Smith learned to do? Write your answer here.**

_____

Jed was very brave. Once, when he was in South Dakota, he was attacked by a very large bear. Jed was almost killed, but a month later he was strong enough to walk.

In the Rocky Mountains, Jed was a trapper. He caught animals and sold them for their fur. There were hundreds of men like Jed. They called themselves mountain men.

The mountain men had to spend a lot of time alone. They would hunt for 11 months. Then, in late summer, they would take the furs to a place where they could sell them.

A mountain man

The most important thing Jed owned was his gun. He used it to shoot animals for food. He also used it to keep large animals away. Next to his gun and his knife, a fur trapper like Jed needed his traps. He needed traps to catch beavers. He sold beaver furs to make a little bit of money.

Making money wasn't the most important thing to mountain men. Just staying alive in the wilderness wasn't easy. There were no doctors and no stores that sold food. Many mountain men learned the skills they needed to live in the Rocky Mountain Region from American Indians who lived there.

Most of the mountain men lived in the Rockies because they loved the mountains. They loved their free outdoor life.

By the early 1840s, the fur business was ending. Many mountain men built houses in the region. Others became guides for wagon trains bringing new **settlers** to the area. Settlers are people who go to live in a new part of a country. Today, there are no mountain men. They are part of the history of the Rocky Mountain Region.

▶ **Why do you think the mountain men were good guides for the new settlers?**

_____

Mountain men lived in the wilderness.

Some American Indian groups built their homes in canyon walls.

American Indians in the Region

The mountain men came to the Rocky Mountain Region in the 1820s. Small groups of American Indians had been living in the region for a long time.

During the 1800s, many new settlers came to the region. The American Indians and the settlers had different ideas about how to use the land. There were many battles. The United States government finally moved the Indians off the land and onto **reservations**. A reservation is land set aside by the government where American Indian groups were made to live. The reservations were often far from where the groups had been living. The land was not good for farming or hunting. Life on reservations was very hard.

Today, some American Indians still live on reservations in the Rocky Mountain Region and in other areas of the country. But American Indians do not have to live on reservations anymore. Like other citizens of the United States, they can live where they choose.

➤ Why was life hard on the early reservations?

_____

Where Do People Live in the Region?

Today, more than 11 million people live in the Rocky Mountain Region. It has the smallest population of all the regions in the United States. As in other regions, most people in the Rocky Mountain Region live in cities. The city with the largest population is Denver, Colorado.

In the 1860s, Denver was a small town. People called **miners** were looking for gold and silver in the area. By the 1880s, a railroad had been built to Denver. More people and businesses moved there. Today, Denver is a major business and transportation center.

Denver, Colorado, is known as the "Mile-High City."

Denver is only ten miles from the Rockies. Temperatures are usually cooler up in the mountains than down on the plains. Look at the **line graph** below. A line graph shows how something changes over time. This line graph shows what the temperatures are like in Denver during the year.

➤ What are the warmest and coldest months in Denver? Write your answer here.

_____

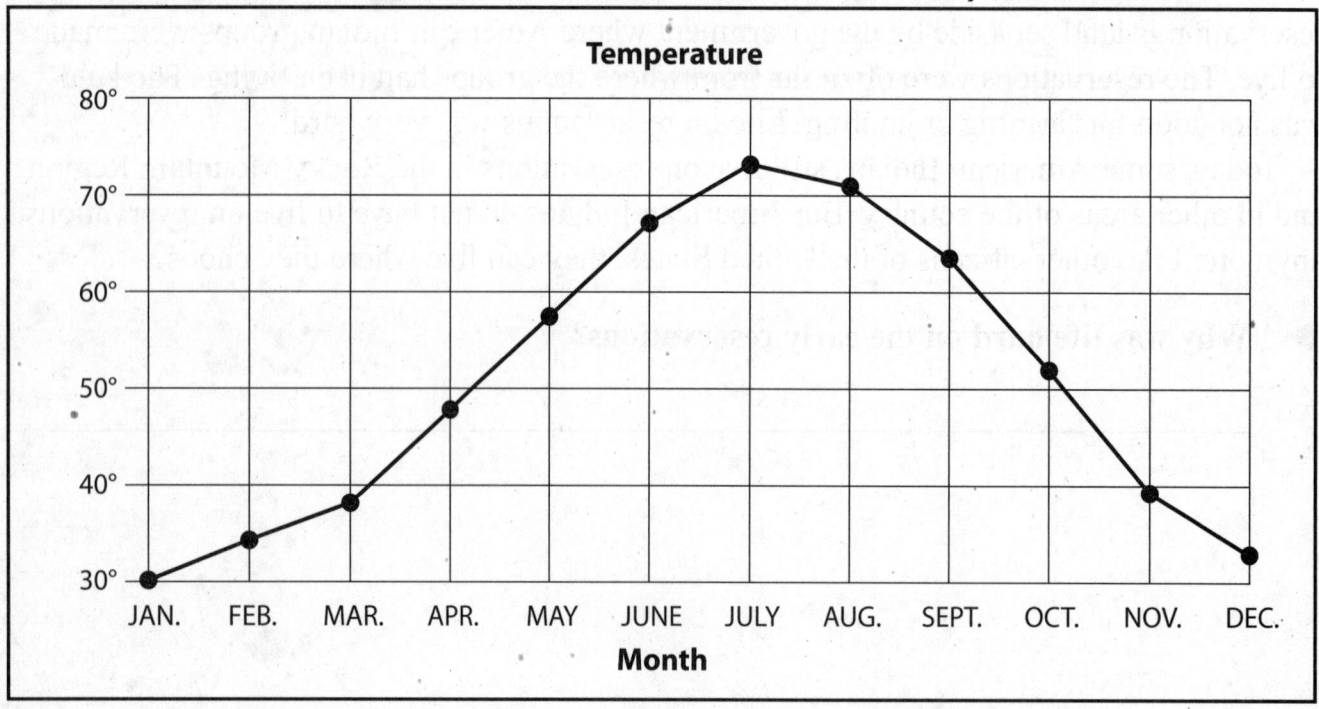

Name _____   Date _____

Another important city is near the Great Salt Lake. It is Salt Lake City.

➤ **Find Salt Lake City on the map on page 70. What state is it in? Write the state here.**

_____

Salt Lake City was started in 1847 by a religious group called the **Mormons**. Like the Pilgrims, they wanted their own land and a place to worship. They worked hard and turned the dry lands into farms. Salt Lake City is still the center of the Mormon religion. More than two out of every three people who live in Utah are Mormons.

Cheyenne, Wyoming, has a population of about 53,000 people. Still, it is one of the biggest cities in the whole Rocky Mountain Region. Every year, people from all over the region visit Cheyenne. Many go to watch the Frontier Days **Rodeo**. A rodeo is a contest for cowboys and cowgirls. At rodeos they get a chance to show the skills they use in their jobs on cattle ranches.

Nevada has the fastest-growing population in the nation. Lots of new businesses have opened in Nevada because running a business there costs less than it does in other states. Many of the new businesses make things such as computers.

Frontier Days Rodeo is a popular event in Cheyenne, Wyoming.

➤ **How do new businesses help the population grow? Write your answer here.**

_____

_____

_____

Name _____ Date _____

Working in the Rocky Mountain Region

There are lots of ranches in the eastern part of the region. The Great Plains come right up to the mountains there. The land there is good for raising cattle.

➤ **Look at the maps on pages 70 and 71. What three states do you think are best for ranching? Write your answer here.**

_____

_____

People in the region also raise sheep. Sheep can live in the mountains, where the land is not good for farming or raising cattle.

People do some farming in the areas that are not in the mountains. Idaho is famous for growing potatoes. Idaho grows more potatoes than any other state! Farmers in Idaho and Montana also grow wheat and other grains.

Raising cattle is an important business in the Rocky Mountain Region.

Name _____ Date _____

Mining is an important industry in this region. About 150 years ago, large amounts of minerals were discovered. Most of our gold and silver comes from this region.

Some of the mountains, lakes, rivers, and canyons are a resource because they are so beautiful. Each year millions of tourists visit the 11 national parks in the region. Park visitors can hike or simply enjoy the scenery.

Many people in the Rocky Mountain Region have tourism jobs. These include car rental agent, souvenir seller, and park ranger. These jobs are also service jobs. As in other regions of the country, there are more service jobs for people than any other kind of job.

➤ **What are three important jobs in the region? Write your answer here.**

_____

_____

Yellowstone National Park in Wyoming contains many natural wonders such as geysers and waterfalls.

Name _____ Date _____

Chapter Checkup

▶ **Darken the circle by the answer that best completes each sentence.**

1. People who go to live in a new part of a country are called
   - Ⓐ guides.
   - Ⓑ mountain men.
   - Ⓒ settlers.
   - Ⓓ miners.

2. Of all the regions in the United States, the Rocky Mountain Region has the
   - Ⓐ most people.
   - Ⓑ fewest people.
   - Ⓒ best land for farming.
   - Ⓓ best land for houses.

3. Most people in the region live
   - Ⓐ in small towns.
   - Ⓑ in cities.
   - Ⓒ on farms.
   - Ⓓ on ranches.

4. In the 1800s, the United States government forced American Indians to move to
   - Ⓐ reservations.
   - Ⓑ cities.
   - Ⓒ farms.
   - Ⓓ national parks.

5. Salt Lake City was begun by a group of settlers called
   - Ⓐ American Indians.
   - Ⓑ cowboys.
   - Ⓒ mountain men.
   - Ⓓ Mormons.

6. Many people in the region have
   - Ⓐ tourism jobs.
   - Ⓑ offshore drilling jobs.
   - Ⓒ deep sea fishing jobs.
   - Ⓓ shipbuilding jobs.

THINKING AND WRITING

Why do so few people live in the Rocky Mountain Region?

_____
_____
_____
_____
_____

Name _____ Date _____

Unit 5 Skill Builder: Reading a Line Graph

Large numbers of settlers first began coming to Nevada in 1859 when silver was discovered there. This line graph shows how Nevada's population has grown.

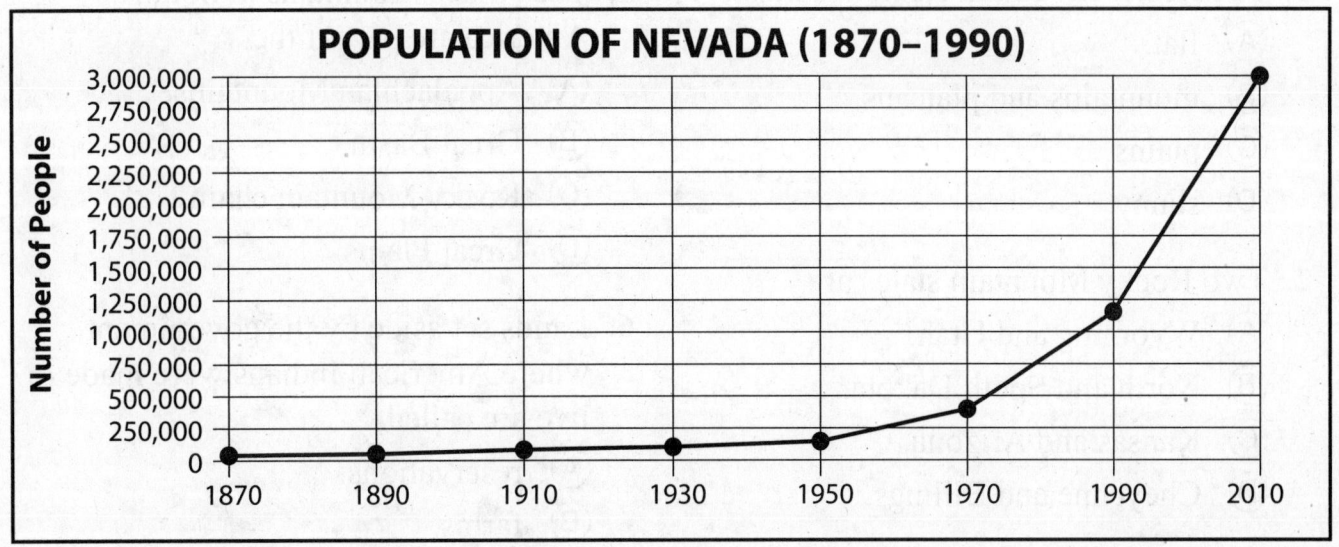

1. Circle the answer that tells what happened to Nevada's population between 1870 and 1990.

    It got bigger. 　　　It stayed the same. 　　　It got smaller.

2. When was Nevada's population about 200,000?

    _____

3. What was the population of Nevada in 1990?

    _____

4. Did the population grow more between 1930 and 1950 or between 1970 and 1990?

    _____

5. How would a line graph look for a town whose population got smaller?

    _____

Name _____ Date _____

Unit 5 Test

➤ **Darken the circle by the answer that best completes each sentence.**

1. The Rocky Mountain Region is mostly
   - Ⓐ flat.
   - Ⓑ mountains and plateaus.
   - Ⓒ plains.
   - Ⓓ sunny.

2. Two Rocky Mountain states are
   - Ⓐ Wyoming and Utah.
   - Ⓑ North and South Dakota.
   - Ⓒ Kansas and Arizona.
   - Ⓓ Cheyenne and Billings.

3. The Great Salt Lake is what is left of
   - Ⓐ a large river.
   - Ⓑ a huge lake.
   - Ⓒ a glacier.
   - Ⓓ the Pacific Ocean.

4. A deep narrow valley formed by rushing water is called
   - Ⓐ a basin.
   - Ⓑ the Continental Divide.
   - Ⓒ a canyon.
   - Ⓓ the highlands.

5. The Andes Mountains in South America are part of the
   - Ⓐ Appalachian Mountains.
   - Ⓑ Great Basin.
   - Ⓒ Rocky Mountain chain.
   - Ⓓ Great Plains.

6. Lands set aside by the government where American Indians were made to live are called
   - Ⓐ reservations.
   - Ⓑ farms.
   - Ⓒ ranches.
   - Ⓓ settlements.

7. The Rocky Mountain Region has many
   - Ⓐ cattle ranches.
   - Ⓑ pig farms.
   - Ⓒ cornfields.
   - Ⓓ chicken farms.

8. Important minerals mined in the Rocky Mountain Region are
   - Ⓐ coal and oil.
   - Ⓑ salt and sand.
   - Ⓒ iron and steel.
   - Ⓓ silver and gold.

THINKING AND WRITING

What kinds of skills did the mountain men need to have?

_____

_____

Name _____ Date _____

Chapter 12: Geography of the Southwest Region

In the last unit, you read about a region that is full of mountains. The Southwest Region has mountains, too, but more than half of the Southwest is flat plains.

States and Cities of the Southwest

There are only four states in the Southwest Region. One of them is the second-biggest state in our nation. Can you find this state on the map below?

➤ **Draw a line from the state capital farthest west to the state capital farthest south.**

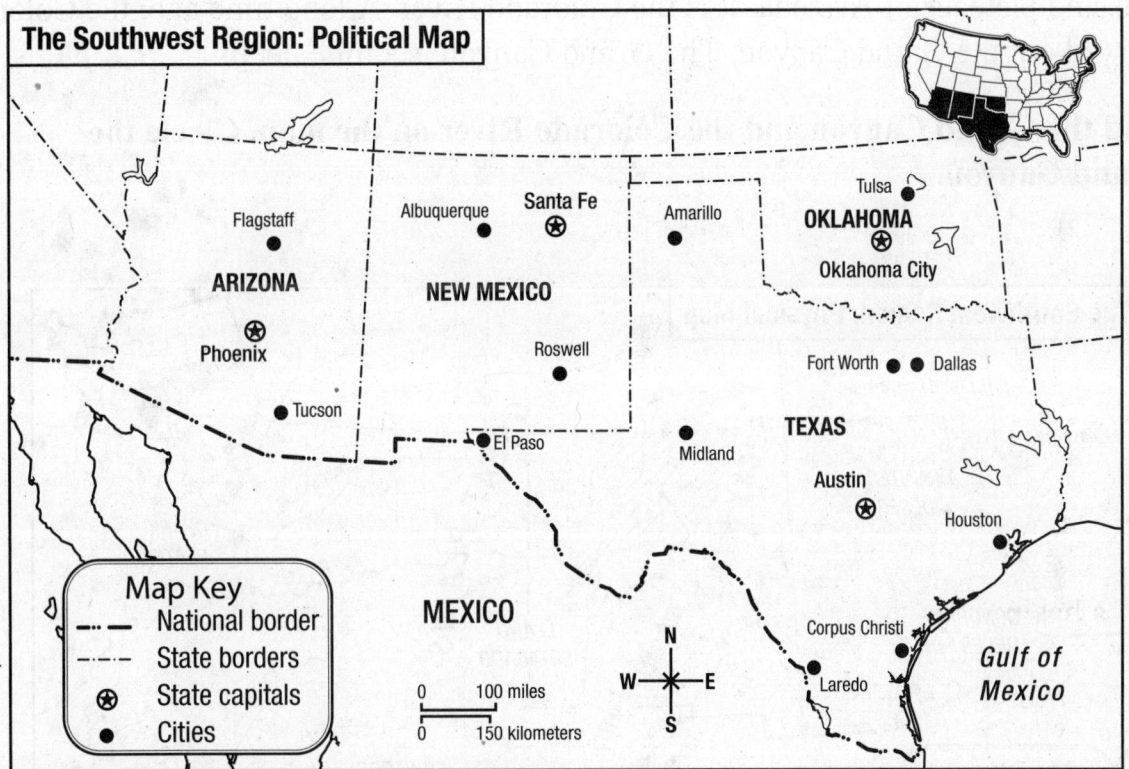

85

Unit 6, Chapter 12
© Houghton Mifflin Harcourt Publishing Company
Core Skills Social Studies, Grade 4

Name _____ Date _____

Land, Rivers, and Climate

The land of the Southwest looks like a set of stairs. The lowest step is the Coastal Plain. Look at the map below. Find the words *Coastal Plain* near the Gulf of Mexico.

The Great Plains are the middle step. They are higher than the Coastal Plains but lower than highlands or mountains.

➤ **Arizona and New Mexico are the top step. Look at the map. What landforms make up these states? Write your answer here.**

_____

There are many rivers on the plains of Texas. There is only one major river in the highlands and plateaus of Arizona. It is the Colorado River. A long time ago, the Colorado River carved out the Grand Canyon. The Grand Canyon is a mile deep!

➤ **Find the Grand Canyon and the Colorado River on the map. Circle the Grand Canyon.**

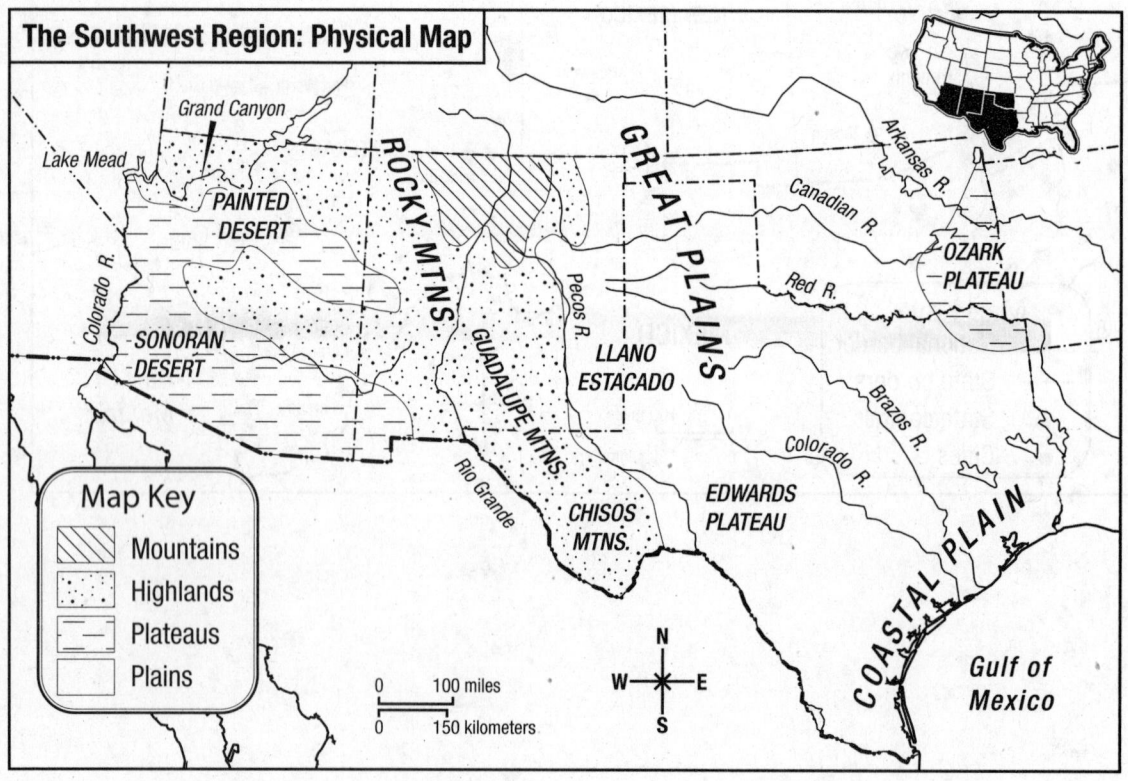

Name _____ Date _____

Parts of the Southwest are known for being hot and sunny. The Southwest is part of the Sunbelt. But this does not mean that the whole region has the same climate. On a day when oranges are growing in the south of Texas, it may be snowing in the north of Texas. Texas is a big state!

➤ **Turn back to the climate map on page 8. Find Texas. How many climate areas does it have? Write your answer here.**

_____

There are **deserts** in the Southwest. Deserts are dry lands with very little rainfall. Deserts in the Southwest can get very hot.

Desert plants have long roots that reach deep into the ground where there is water. Desert animals hide from the strong sun. They look for food and water at night.

People have found ways to bring water from far away to the desert. Watering crops by bringing water to an area where it is in short supply is called **irrigation**. With the help of irrigation, farmers can grow cotton, vegetables, and other crops.

The Colorado River began carving the Grand Canyon about 6,000,000 years ago.

Name _____ Date _____

Chapter Checkup

▶ **Darken the circle by the answer that best completes each sentence.**

1. More than half of the land in the Southwest is
   - Ⓐ mountains.
   - Ⓑ plateaus.
   - Ⓒ flat plains.
   - Ⓓ highlands.

2. The largest state in the Southwest is
   - Ⓐ Arizona.
   - Ⓑ New Mexico.
   - Ⓒ Oklahoma.
   - Ⓓ Texas.

3. Most of the rivers in the Southwest are in the
   - Ⓐ mountains.
   - Ⓑ plains.
   - Ⓒ deserts.
   - Ⓓ highlands.

4. The Grand Canyon was carved by
   - Ⓐ the Colorado River.
   - Ⓑ the desert.
   - Ⓒ American Indians.
   - Ⓓ irrigation.

5. Deserts are lands that have very little
   - Ⓐ warm air.
   - Ⓑ mountains.
   - Ⓒ rainfall.
   - Ⓓ sunshine.

6. When farmers bring water to dry land from far away, it is called
   - Ⓐ a coastal plain.
   - Ⓑ irrigation.
   - Ⓒ farming.
   - Ⓓ a desert.

THINKING AND WRITING

Would you rather visit the Grand Canyon or the desert? Give your reasons.

_____
_____
_____
_____
_____
_____

Name _____   Date _____

Chapter 13: People of the Southwest Region

Many people settled in the Southwest in the past. Today, many people are still moving there. But who were the very first people to live in the region? American Indian groups arrived thousands of years ago.

Long Ago: The Comanche

The Comanche once ruled the plains. They were great hunters and fighters. They lived in small groups. They moved to find food. In summer they followed the herds of deer and buffalo across the plains. They dried some of the meat to eat during the winter.

For hundreds of years, Comanche children learned the same lessons. Fathers taught sons to hunt. Mothers taught daughters to prepare food and clothing from buffalo and deer.

▶ **Why do you think the Comanche dried meat for the winter? Write your answer here.**

_____

_____

Then, about 300 years ago, a great change began. Other people arrived from Spain. They were ranchers who came to raise cattle. They brought horses with them to the Southwest.

Once the Comanche had horses, their way of life changed. They became great riders. It was easier to follow and hunt the buffalo herds.

American Indians were the first to live in the Southwest.

89

Unit 6, Chapter 13

© Houghton Mifflin Harcourt Publishing Company

Core Skills Social Studies, Grade 4

Name _____   Date _____

Horses also made the Comanche strong in war. On horseback they were able to win more battles. By 1800, they ruled a large part of the Southwest.

Soon thousands of settlers moved to Texas. They moved there because they wanted to build farms and ranches.

The Comanche tried to make the settlers leave. Then United States soldiers attacked Comanche camps. The fighting went on for a long time. But the guns and soldiers did not beat the Comanche.

The Comanche were beaten by sickness. The settlers brought sicknesses from Europe. The Comanche had never had these sicknesses before. Thousands died. In the early 1800s, there were 30,000 Comanche. Fifty years later there were only half as many.

▶ **About how many Comanche were there in 1850? Write your answer here.**

_____

The Comanche were also beaten by the buffalo hunters with guns. The hunters killed the animals that the Comanche needed for food and clothing. These hunters killed as many buffalo as they could. In just a few years, the great buffalo herds were gone.

In 1875, the last Comanche were moved to a reservation. They were no longer allowed to travel across the plains.

▶ **What two "enemies" hurt the Comanche most? Write your answer here.**

_____

The Comanche needed the buffalo for food and clothing.

Who Are the People of the Region?

Over 31 million people live in the four southwestern states. There are more American Indians and Mexican Americans in the Southwest Region than in any other region.

American Indian groups arrived in the Southwest long ago. The Navajo and Pueblo were living in the Southwest by the year 1300.

➤ **What groups of people lived in the Southwest Region about 700 years ago? Write your answer here.**

_____

During the early 1800s, most of what is now Oklahoma was known as Indian Territory. The United States government had set aside this land for American Indians. Many American Indians from different parts of the country had been forced to settle in Indian Territory.

The Oklahoma Land Rush

By the 1880s, many settlers had come and set up cattle ranches all around Indian Territory. The settlers told the government they wanted the land in Indian Territory. The government told the American Indians they could sell the land. Many American Indians sold their land in Oklahoma.

In 1889, the government held a Land Rush—a race to claim land that had once been Indian Territory. Over 50,000 settlers entered Oklahoma in one day to get the land.

Today, a large number of American Indians live in the Southwest. Many live on reservations in the region. The Navajo reservation covers parts of Arizona, New Mexico, and Utah. It is the largest American Indian reservation in the United States.

Name _____ Date _____

People from Spain arrived in the Southwest in the 1500s. They built a colony in New Mexico in 1598, more than 20 years before the Pilgrims landed in the Northeast.

Spanish-speaking people have lived in the Southwest for hundreds of years. Until about 150 years ago, most of the Southwest was part of Mexico or a colony of Spain. All through the 1900s, thousands of Mexicans moved to the Southwest. Today, Mexican Americans make up one-fourth of the population of the Southwest.

An adobe house in Santa Fe, New Mexico

▶ **Look at the time line at the bottom of the page. A time line is a line that shows a number of years. Marks on the line stand for events that happened during those years.**

Some events of the Southwest Region are shown on the time line. This time line covers 700 years. Each small part of the time line stands for 100 years.

Write 1889 where it belongs on the time line. Draw a line to the words that go with it.

How many years passed between the time when the first Spanish colony was started and the Land Rush? Write your answer here.

_____

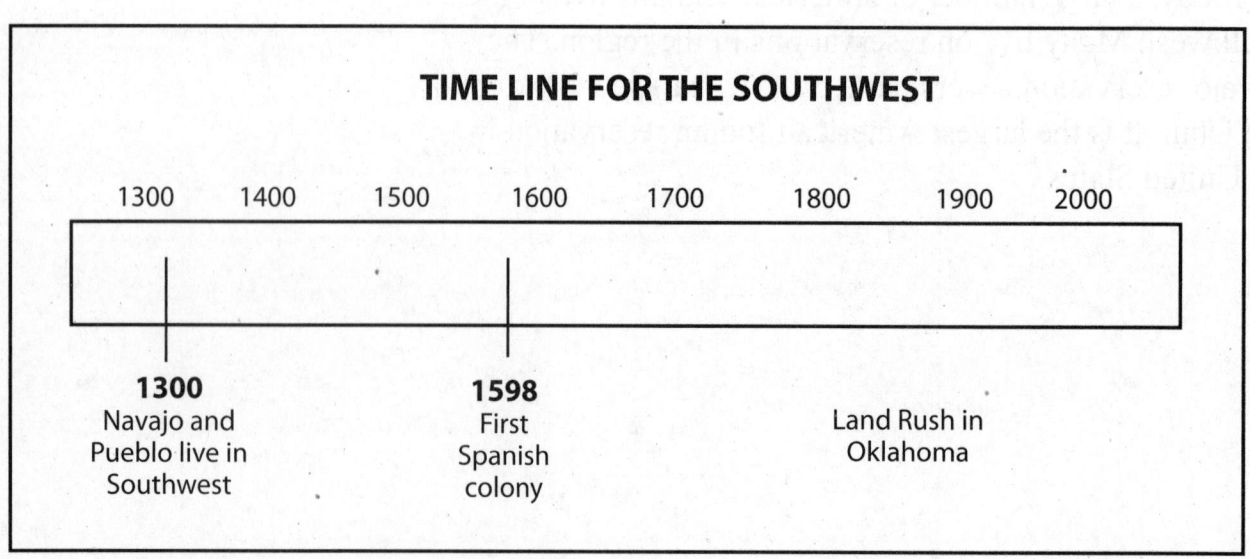

Where Do People Live in the Region?

You have learned that there are deserts in the Southwest. There is not much water in the desert. Most people in the Southwest live in cities.

The city of San Antonio is by a river on the Texas plains. It began as a farming village. Because the weather is so warm there, farmers grow crops all year round.

Houston, Texas, is on several bayous. A **bayou** is a creek or small river. Buffalo Bayou was dug out to form the Houston Ship Channel. Houston became a major port after oil was discovered in Texas.

Oil is very important to many of the cities in the Southwest. Tulsa, Oklahoma, was an American Indian farming village. After oil was discovered there, it became a big business center. Now more than 350 oil companies have their offices there.

➤ **What business is important to both Texas and Oklahoma? Write your answer here.**

_____

Houston, Texas, is located on several bayous.

Some southwestern cities were built near old roads or trails. Many of these had been used by travelers for centuries. The city of Albuquerque started along a road. Later a railroad was built across New Mexico. Now Albuquerque is the largest city in the state.

▶ **How do you think the railroad helped Albuquerque grow? Write your answer here.**

_____

_____

Oklahoma City was one of the first towns settled during the Land Rush of 1889. Oil was discovered under the city in 1928. The city grew quickly after that.

Many cities in the Southwest have Spanish names. That is usually because they were started by the early Spanish settlers. Some houses in southwestern cities look like houses in Mexico. People often eat Mexican food and play Mexican music. The Southwest also has the largest Mexican American population in the country.

An American Indian woman in traditional dress

Name _____   Date _____

Traveling in the Southwest Region

How do drivers find the way to places they have never been before? Most of the time, they use road maps. Some maps also show places of special interest to travelers.

For example, pretend you're traveling through Oklahoma. You would like to find a campground where you can spend the night.

▶ **Look at the road map below. It shows part of Oklahoma. Look at the map key. Find the symbol for campground. Circle the campground you would reach by traveling on Interstate Highway 40.**

Now pretend you are traveling from the town of Chandler to the town of Goldsby. Find the town of Chandler in the northeast corner of the road map. Next, find the town of Goldsby. Now trace the roads you would follow to drive from Chandler to Goldsby.

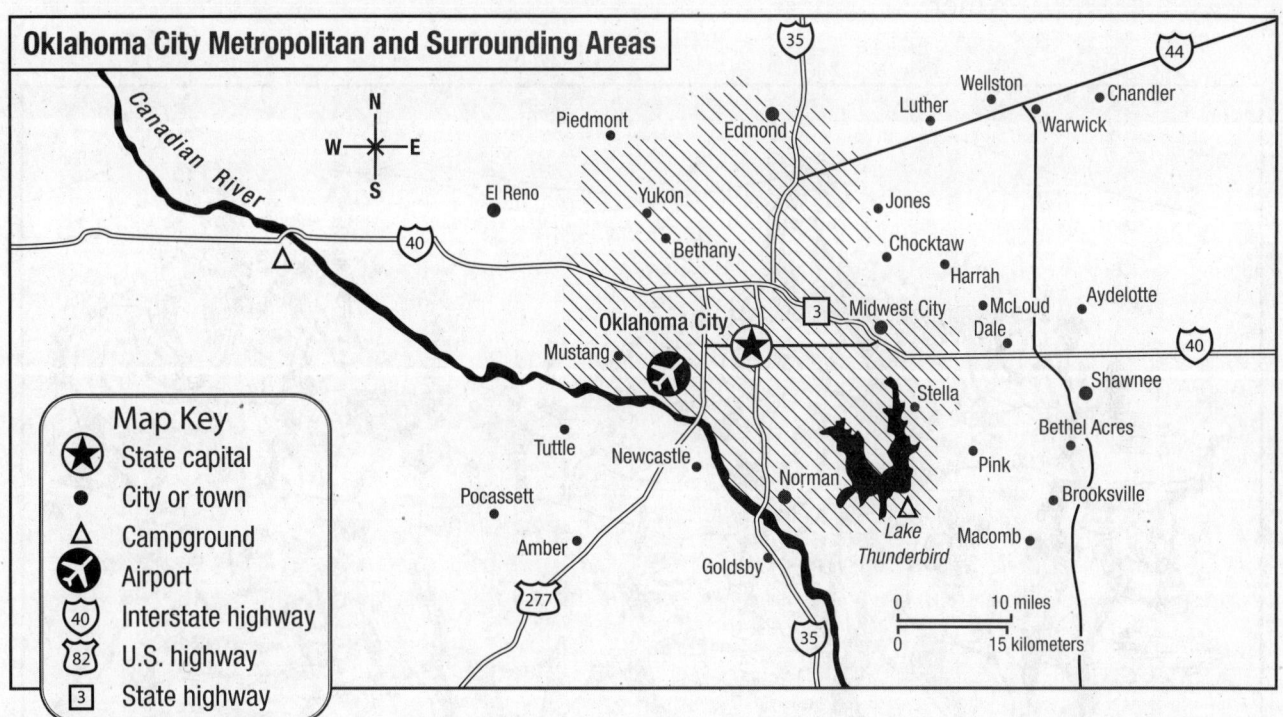

Name _____ Date _____

Working in the Southwest Region

Ranching was the first business in the Southwest. People from Spain had started raising cattle in Texas by the 1700s. Ranching became more important as the United States grew. One Texas ranch grew bigger than the state of Rhode Island!

There were no railroads in Texas in the mid-1800s. So ranchers had to walk the cattle north to cities where there were railroads. These cattle drives were hundreds of miles long and very dangerous.

In the late 1800s, railroads were built to Texas. The long cattle drives were over. But cattle ranching is still an important business in Texas today.

➤ **Why do you think railroads ended the need for the cattle drives? Write your answer here.**

_____

_____

A cattle drive

Name _____ Date _____

Around 1900 a new business grew up in the Southwest—oil. The states of Texas and Oklahoma produce a lot of oil. Oil is used to make gasoline and other products. Cars, planes, and ships need gas and oil to be able to move. Homes and buildings are heated with oil. Plastics and many other products are made from oil.

Usually, oil is found far under the ground. Special wells are needed to pump it out. Then it must go to a place called a **refinery**. In a refinery, the oil is cleaned and made into different products.

Today there are many jobs in the oil business. What jobs will the Southwest have in the future? New jobs usually come from **research**. *Research* means "studying things and finding out about them." Research is often done by businesses and universities. Research scientists often solve problems by finding better ways to do things. For example, we know we have to be careful with our natural resources.

One thing researchers in the Southwest work on is new ways to use less oil. They study other types of energy that can be used. Have you ever heard of **solar energy**? Solar energy uses the heat of the sun instead of oil to heat homes.

Oil pumps are a common sight in Texas and Oklahoma.

➤ **If you did research, what would you want to study? Write your answer here.**

_____

Many people in the Southwest have service jobs. Like other regions of the United States, the Southwest needs teachers, doctors, salespeople, and other service workers.

Name _____ Date _____

Chapter Checkup

▶ **Darken the circle by the answer that best completes each sentence.**

1. The first people to live in the Southwest were
   - Ⓐ Spaniards.
   - Ⓑ American Indians.
   - Ⓒ settlers.
   - Ⓓ Mexican Americans.

2. The Comanche were able to hunt better when they got
   - Ⓐ sick.
   - Ⓑ reservations.
   - Ⓒ settlers.
   - Ⓓ horses.

3. The largest American Indian reservation in the United States is that of the
   - Ⓐ Comanche.
   - Ⓑ Pueblo.
   - Ⓒ Sioux.
   - Ⓓ Navajo.

4. To get their cattle to market, ranchers had cattle drives to get to
   - Ⓐ Texas.
   - Ⓑ railroads.
   - Ⓒ Mexico.
   - Ⓓ rivers.

5. The states of Texas and Oklahoma produce a lot of
   - Ⓐ soil.
   - Ⓑ steel.
   - Ⓒ electricity.
   - Ⓓ oil.

6. One thing research scientists do is
   - Ⓐ look for gold.
   - Ⓑ move to Oklahoma.
   - Ⓒ find better ways to do things.
   - Ⓓ go on cattle drives.

| THINKING AND WRITING |

What job in the Southwest Region sounds the most interesting to you? Explain why.

_____

_____

_____

_____

Name _____ Date _____

Unit 6 Skill Builder: Reading a Road Map

Look at the road map of part of New Mexico. There is often more than one road you can take to the same place. Road maps can show you the shortest way.

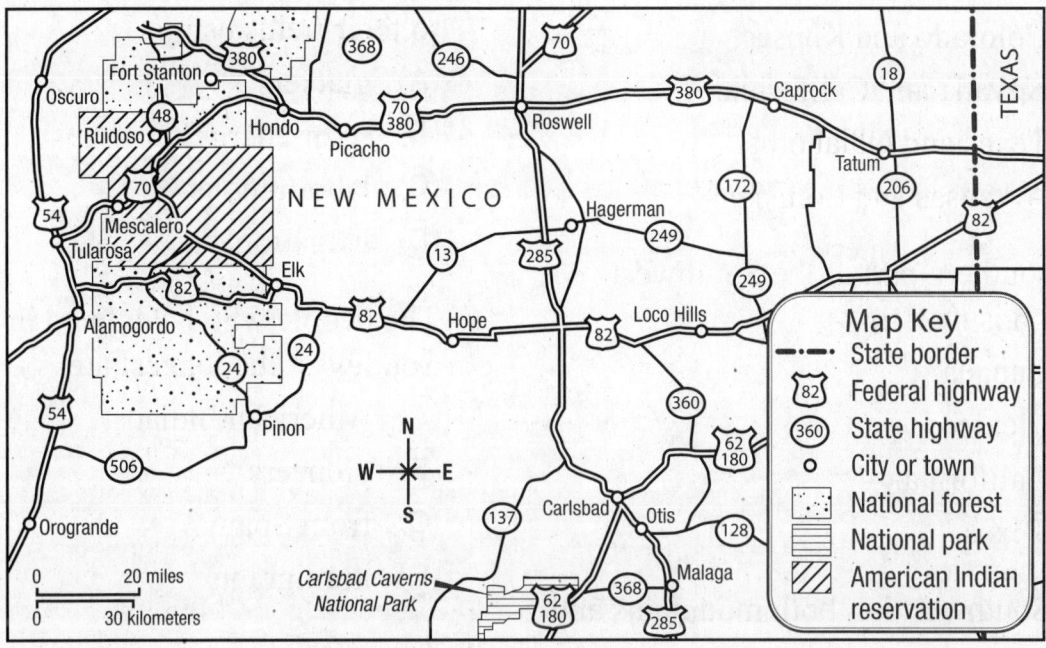

1. What two kinds of roads appear on the map?

   _____

2. Which federal highway goes through the Mescalero Apache Indian Reservation?

   _____

3. What road would you take to travel from Roswell to Caprock? What direction would you travel?

   _____

4. Someone tells you about the interesting caves at Carlsbad Caverns National Park. List the highways you would take from Caprock to Carlsbad Caverns.

   _____

Name _____   Date _____

Unit 6 Test

▶ **Darken the circle by the answer that best completes each sentence.**

1. Two states in the Southwest are
   - Ⓐ Colorado and Kansas.
   - Ⓑ Nevada and California.
   - Ⓒ Texas and Oklahoma.
   - Ⓓ Arkansas and Louisiana.

2. The southern part of the Southwest Region is next to
   - Ⓐ Canada.
   - Ⓑ Mexico.
   - Ⓒ California.
   - Ⓓ Texas.

3. The Southwest has both mountains and
   - Ⓐ flat plains.
   - Ⓑ an ocean coast.
   - Ⓒ salt lakes.
   - Ⓓ large islands.

4. Lands that get very little rain are called
   - Ⓐ deserts.
   - Ⓑ highlands.
   - Ⓒ plains.
   - Ⓓ canyons.

5. Farmers in the Southwest bring water to their fields using
   - Ⓐ glaciers.
   - Ⓑ solar energy.
   - Ⓒ labor unions.
   - Ⓓ irrigation.

6. The people who have lived in the Southwest the longest are
   - Ⓐ American Indians.
   - Ⓑ pioneers.
   - Ⓒ from Spain.
   - Ⓓ immigrants.

7. Tulsa, Oklahoma, became a big business center after the discovery of
   - Ⓐ gold.
   - Ⓑ silver.
   - Ⓒ solar energy.
   - Ⓓ oil.

8. Long cattle drives ended when people built
   - Ⓐ ships.
   - Ⓑ refineries.
   - Ⓒ railroads.
   - Ⓓ reservations.

THINKING AND WRITING

Which would be a better place to start a cattle ranch: the mountains of Colorado or the plains of Texas? Explain your choice.

Name _____   Date _____

Chapter 14: Geography of the Pacific Region

The Pacific Region is the only region where two of the states are separated from the rest of the United States. That is why its geography is the most varied and unusual of any region.

The West Coast States

Three of the Pacific Region states are called the West Coast states. Find them on the left map. Trace the edges of the three states with a pencil or crayon.

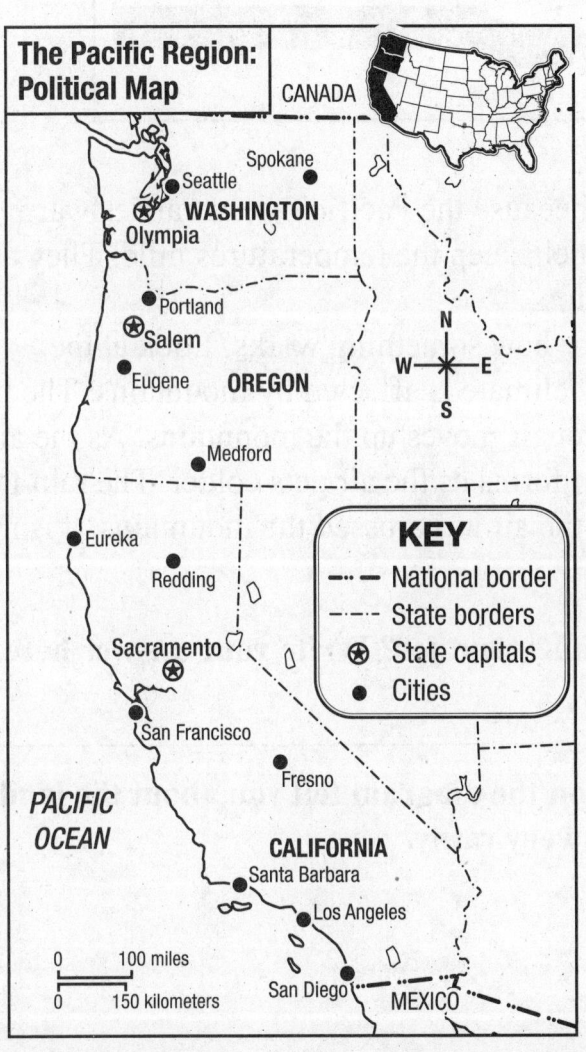
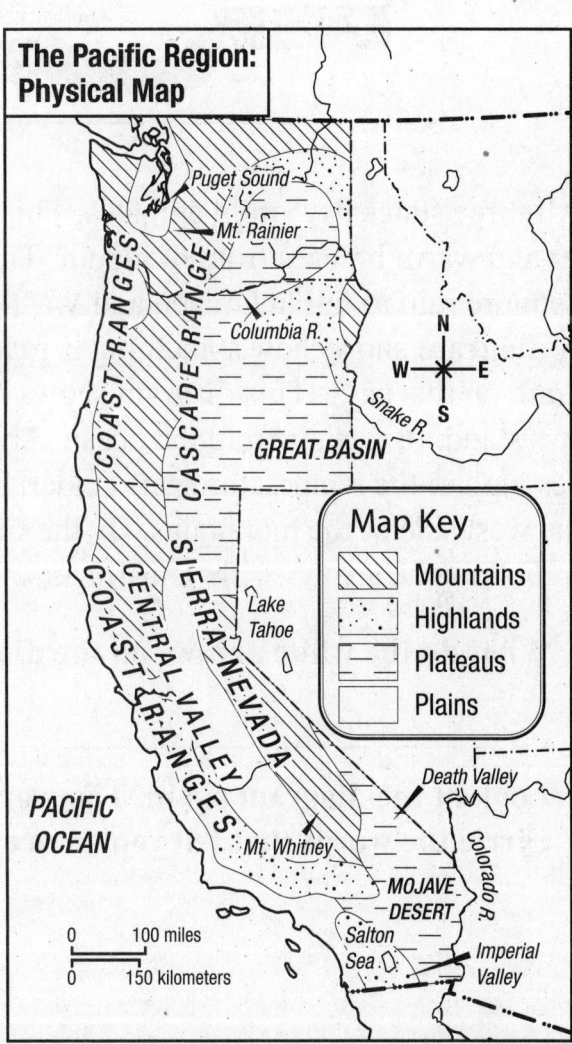

101

Unit 7, Chapter 14
Core Skills Social Studies, Grade 4

Name _____ Date _____

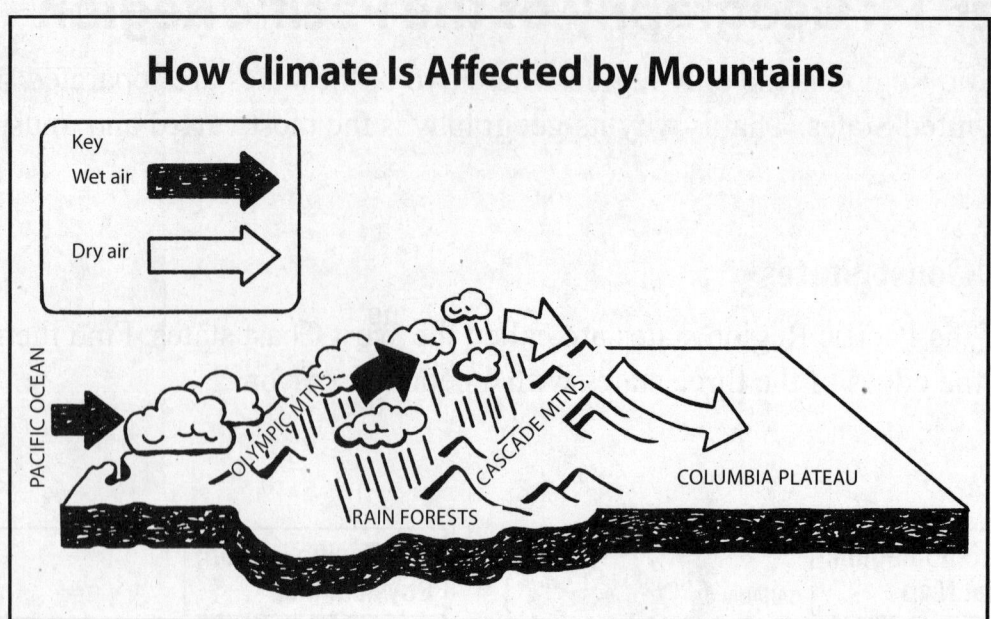

All three states have mild climates. This is because the Pacific Ocean carries warm water and warm breezes from the south. They help keep the temperatures mild. They also cause more rain to fall in Oregon and Washington.

A **diagram** shows how something is made or how something works. Look at the diagram on this page. This diagram shows how climate is affected by mountains. The black arrows stand for wet air from the ocean. The wet air moves up the mountains. As the air moves higher, the temperature gets colder. Rain forms as the air gets colder. The rain falls on the west side of the mountains. By the time the air has crossed the mountains, it is much drier. Follow the arrows with your finger.

➤ **What do the white arrows on the diagram stand for? Write your answer here.**

_____

Look at the diagram again. The words on the diagram tell you about the land. Circle the words that tell you an area is very rainy.

Earthquakes

People were sound asleep when the ground began to shake. Some people were thrown out of their beds! Lamps fell and set fire to houses. In a few hours, 3,000 people had died and 28,000 buildings had been destroyed. This happened in the **earthquake** that hit San Francisco, California, in 1906. An earthquake is a strong shaking of the ground.

In the United States, most earthquakes happen in the Pacific Region. This is because two gigantic areas of land meet there. One is under the Pacific Ocean. The other is under the West Coast. If one of them moves against the other, it causes the ground nearby to shake. The place where the two land areas meet is called a **fault**.

Most earthquakes in the Pacific Region are very small. The strongest earthquake in North America took place in Alaska in 1964. Scientists have equipment to measure how strong earthquakes are. They use a special scale called a Richter scale to measure the earthquake. The highest Richter scale ever measured was 8.9. The 1906 San Francisco earthquake measured 8.3.

The San Francisco earthquake of 1906 caused great destruction.

▶ **What is an earthquake? Write your answer here.**

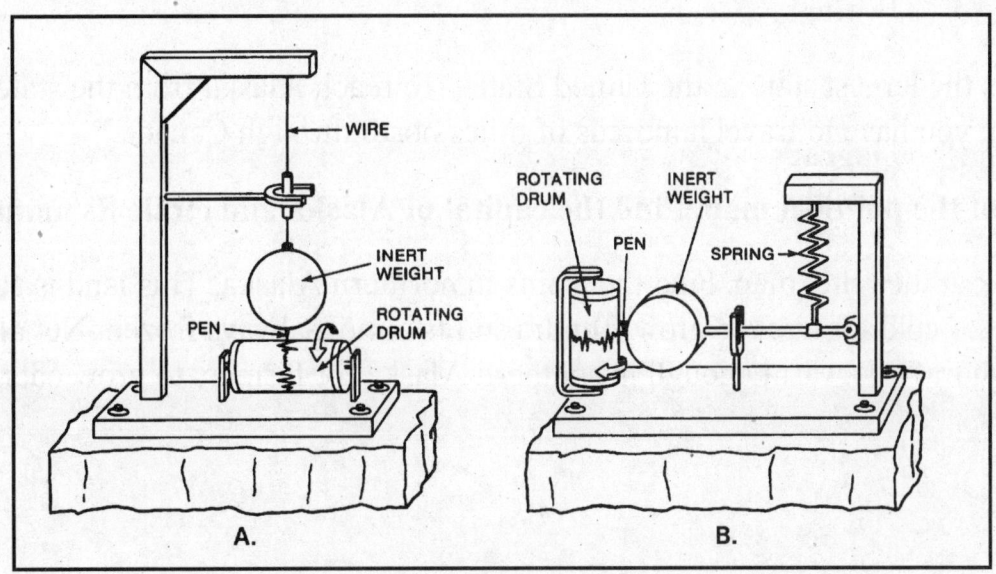

Seismographs measure and record Earth's vibrations.

Name _____ Date _____

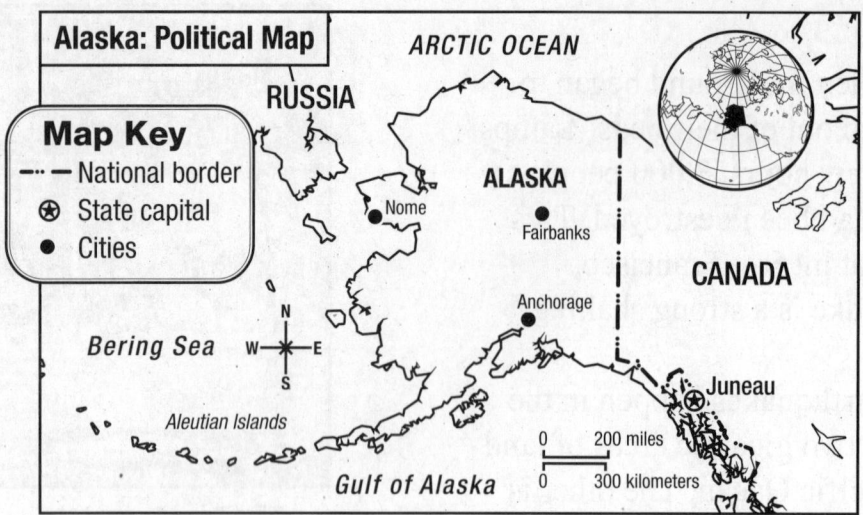

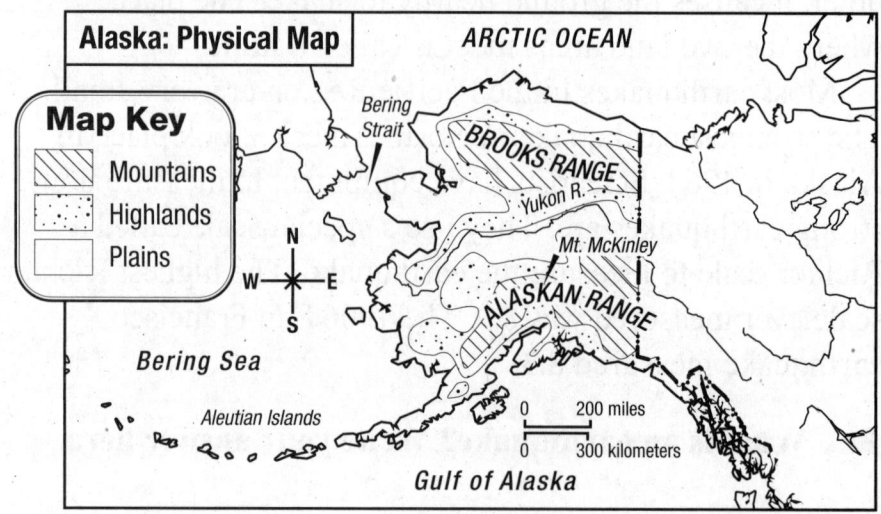

Alaska

Alaska is the largest state in the United States. To reach Alaska from the state of Washington, you have to travel hundreds of miles north through Canada.

▶ **Look at the political map. Find the capital of Alaska and circle its name.**

Now look at the relief map. Find the plains in northern Alaska. This land is **tundra**—land that is too cold for trees to grow. Tundra soil is almost always frozen. Not all of Alaska is tundra. It is warm enough in southern Alaska for farmers to grow oats, barley, and potatoes.

Name _____ Date _____

Hawaii

Hawaii is farther west and farther south than any other state. It is hundreds of miles out in the Pacific Ocean. Hawaii is known for its mild, pleasant climate. Look at the top map. Find the islands of Hawaii.

➤ **Look at the physical map of the islands of Hawaii. Compare it to the physical map of Alaska on page 104. How are the two states alike? Write your answer here.**

_____

Hawaii's mountains are not like regular mountains. In fact, the islands of Hawaii were formed long ago by **volcanoes**. Volcanoes are openings in the crust of the earth through which melting rock, dust, ash, and hot gases are thrown up. The hot rock is called **lava**. When volcanoes **erupt**, they shoot lava into the air.

Millions of years ago, volcanoes under the Pacific Ocean erupted. The hardened lava formed the Hawaiian Islands. Even today, Hawaii's volcanoes erupt from time to time.

Hawaii has several active volcanoes.

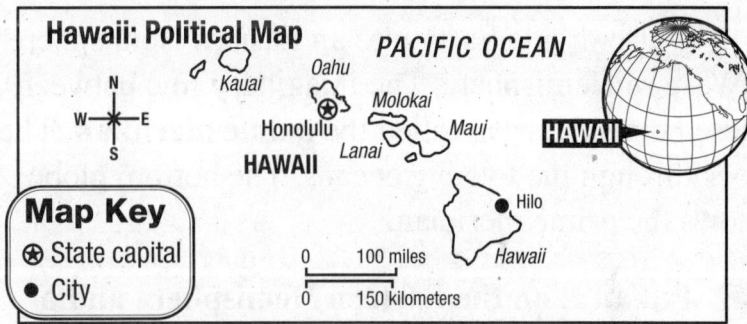

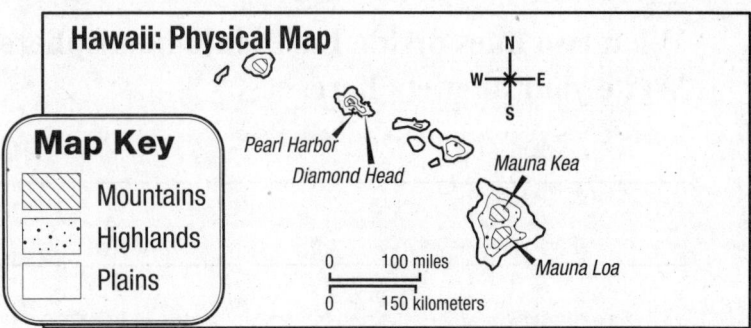

105

Unit 7, Chapter 14

Name _____ Date _____

Dividing Earth

The Pacific Region states are spread over a large part of Earth. Look at the top globe on this page. Find the islands of Hawaii on the northern and western side of the globe. How do we know where north or west is? Earth looks like a big ball, and a ball does not have a top or bottom. Look at the first globe again. Earth turns on an imaginary **axis**, or center line. The axis goes from the North Pole to the South Pole.

We divide Earth into a northern half and a southern half. These halves are called **hemispheres**. The imaginary line where the two halves meet is called the **equator**. The globe in the middle shows the two hemispheres.

➤ Put an <u>N</u> on the Northern Hemisphere and an <u>S</u> on the Southern Hemisphere.

We also divide Earth into an Eastern Hemisphere and a Western Hemisphere. The imaginary line between these hemispheres is called the **prime meridian**. The line goes through the two big oceans. The bottom globe shows the prime meridian.

➤ Put an <u>E</u> on the Eastern Hemisphere and a <u>W</u> on the Western Hemisphere.

What two lines divide Earth into hemispheres? Write your answers here.

_____

_____

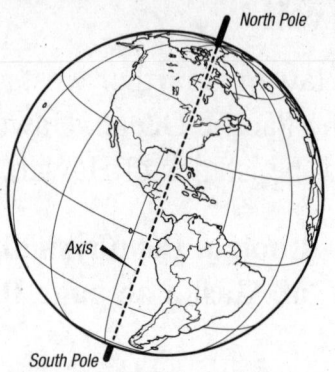

Earth spins on an imaginary axis. The North and South poles are the two ends of the axis.

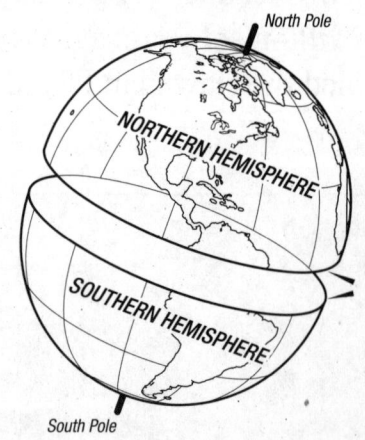

If we could cut Earth into a northern half and a southern half, it would look like this.

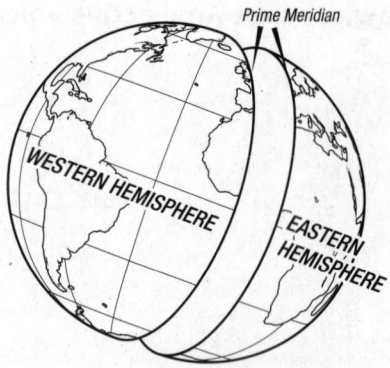

If we could cut Earth into an eastern half and a western half, it would look like this.

Name _____ Date _____

Chapter Checkup

➤ Darken the circle by the answer that best completes each sentence.

1. The West Coast states of the Pacific Region are
   - Ⓐ California, Oregon, and Alaska.
   - Ⓑ California, Oregon, and Washington.
   - Ⓒ Oregon, Hawaii, and Alaska.
   - Ⓓ Washington, Oregon, and Alaska.

2. Warm Pacific Ocean breezes help make the climate of the West Coast states
   - Ⓐ cold.
   - Ⓑ hot.
   - Ⓒ dry.
   - Ⓓ mild.

3. As wet air gets colder, it produces
   - Ⓐ deserts.
   - Ⓑ rain.
   - Ⓒ sunshine.
   - Ⓓ warm air.

4. The land in Alaska that is too cold to grow trees is called
   - Ⓐ Canada.
   - Ⓑ snow.
   - Ⓒ tundra.
   - Ⓓ a volcano.

5. The islands of Hawaii were formed by
   - Ⓐ earthquakes.
   - Ⓑ tourists.
   - Ⓒ volcanoes.
   - Ⓓ tundras.

6. The northern and southern halves of Earth are called the
   - Ⓐ prime meridian.
   - Ⓑ fault.
   - Ⓒ hemispheres.
   - Ⓓ axis.

THINKING AND WRITING

Suppose you were going to move to Alaska or Hawaii. Which state would you choose? Explain your answer.

_____
_____
_____
_____

Name _____   Date _____

Chapter 15: People of the Pacific Region

Gold was discovered in California in 1848. People hurried there from all over. Here is a diary a gold hunter might have written.

Long Ago: The Gold Rush

20 October 1849 We finally got here, but it took us nearly four months. It was hard crossing the Rocky Mountains in a covered wagon. Our camp is called Rich Gulch. Many people are here already.

25 October 1849 My brother Jim and I got some land of our own. One man at Yuba River got 30 pounds of gold from his piece of land. So far we have only found a few dollars worth of gold. Everything costs a lot here.

24 November 1849 Most gold here is dust or tiny flakes. To find it, you put a handful of sand in a wash pan. Then you scoop up lots of water and move the pan in a circle to keep the sand moving. Gold is heavier, so it goes to the bottom. It is very hard work, and we are not finding much gold.

2 February 1850 Today I came back from San Francisco with food and tools. Right away, people tried to buy them from me. People paid me in gold dust. I got more gold selling supplies than we found in the river in three months! Tomorrow we are going back to San Francisco to buy more supplies.

Panning for gold

➤ **Why were so many people at Rich Gulch camp? Write your answer here.**

Who Are the People of the Pacific Region?

The Pacific Region has as great a mixture of people and ways of life as you can find anywhere in the United States. People have moved to the region from all over the world. Many American Indians, Hispanics, and Asian Americans live in the Pacific Region.

American Indians came to the West Coast area thousands of years ago. Then Spanish colonists and Mexican Americans moved there. During the 1800s, pioneers from the East began moving to the West. At that time the West was known as the **frontier**. A frontier is the farthest edge of a country, where few settlers live.

Most pioneers headed for California or Oregon. Pioneers gathered at Independence, Missouri, where trails to the California, Oregon, and Washington regions began. Back then, the trails were really only tracks in the ground made by covered wagons that had traveled the trail earlier. The trip from Independence to Oregon on the Oregon Trail took six months! Large "trains" of covered wagons made the hard trip across deep rivers, deserts, and the Rocky Mountains. Often, the travelers ran out of food and water and got sick. Even though the trip was dangerous, by 1890 so much of the West had become settled that the United States government announced that the West was no longer a frontier.

▶ **Why do you think pioneers wanted to make the hard journey to the West Coast?**

_____

_____

Pioneers traveled by covered wagon.

Many groups of American Indians, such as the Modoc and Yakima, lived near the West Coast. Before the settlers came, the American Indian groups fished, hunted, and used the trees of the forests to build boats and houses. The American Indians of the Pacific Region had many natural resources they could use.

When settlers and miners arrived, things changed. The settlers and the American Indians fought about how to use the land. Later, the government forced American Indian groups to go to reservations.

The Modoc was one group that fought against having to move to a reservation. But the government moved the Modoc to a reservation in Oregon. A chief named Kintpuash led a group of 80 families back to their old hunting grounds in California. The army tried to force them back to the reservation. For five long months, a small group of Modoc fought the soldiers. The Modoc finally lost the battle. They were moved to a reservation in Oklahoma.

The Yakima and many other Pacific Region American Indian groups still live in the West Coast states. Other American Indian groups such as the Inuit, Aleut, and Tlingit live in Alaska.

This picture shows how the Tlingit of Alaska lived long ago. Their large plank houses provided shelter for many related families.

▶ **Why do you think the Modoc went back to California? Write your answer here.**

_____
_____
_____
_____
_____
_____
_____

Remember that during the 1800s most immigrants to the eastern part of the United States came from countries in Europe. Immigrants from Europe came to the West, too. They hoped to find gold or good land there. But immigration was also different in the West Coast area. In the middle of the 1800s, news of gold in California reached China. China is a country in Asia, which is across the Pacific Ocean. Immigrants from China came to California to look for gold. Because so many settlers were going west, railroad companies wanted to build railroads that would stretch all the way from the East Coast to the West Coast. Thousands of Chinese immigrants helped build the railroads.

▶ **Look at the time line below. What was the first West Coast state? Write your answer here.**

_____

Cable cars are a popular attraction in San Francisco, California.

TIME LINE OF EVENTS: WEST COAST

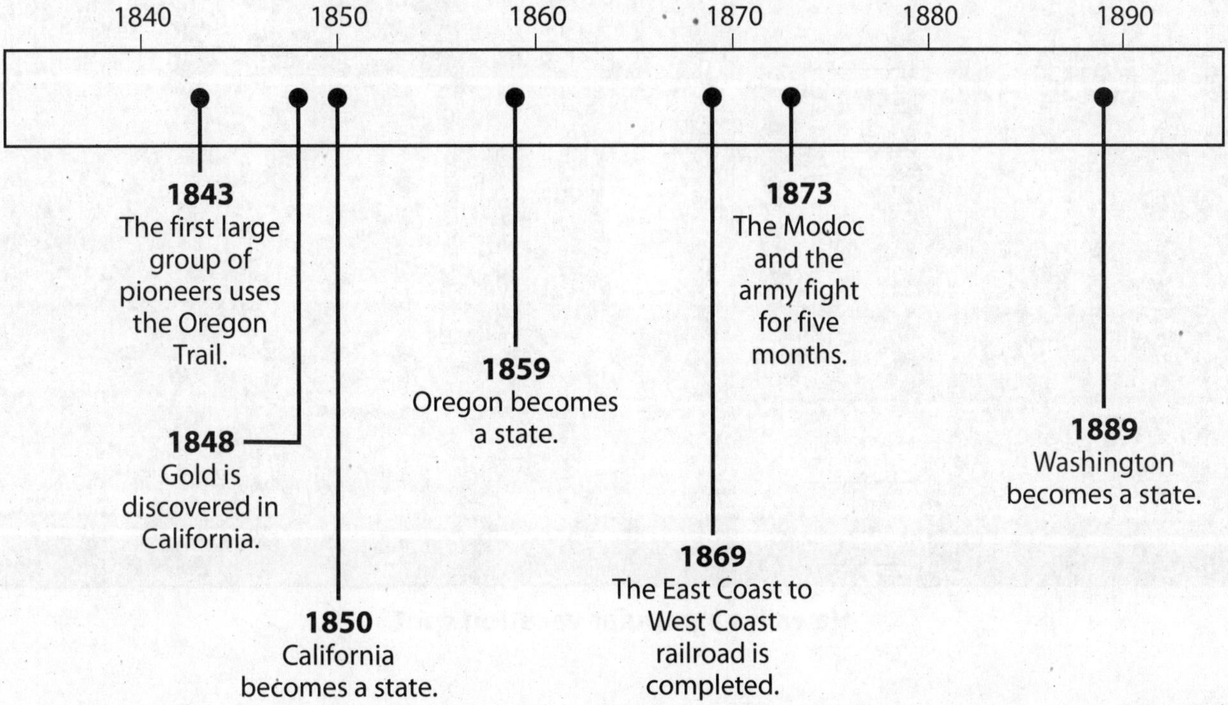

1840 1850 1860 1870 1880 1890

1843 The first large group of pioneers uses the Oregon Trail.

1848 Gold is discovered in California.

1850 California becomes a state.

1859 Oregon becomes a state.

1869 The East Coast to West Coast railroad is completed.

1873 The Modoc and the army fight for five months.

1889 Washington becomes a state.

Where Do People Live in the Pacific Region?

About 45 million people live in the Pacific Region. Alaska is the largest state in the United States, but few people live there. California has the biggest population of all the states.

➤ **Why do you think Alaska has so few people?**

_____

Besides the Pacific Region states, there are hundreds of Pacific Islands in the region. The United States has been closely tied to many of these islands, offering them aid and protection. Some, like the Marshall Islands, have since become independent nations. Others, like Guam, the Northern Marianas, and American Samoa, are U.S. territories.

Honolulu is the largest city in Hawaii. It has one of the best harbors in the world. Because it is in the middle of the Pacific Ocean, Honolulu has become a busy and important port. In the past, ships going to and from Asia stopped there for fresh water and food.

Hawaii is a popular vacation spot.

Name _____   Date _____

The climate is very different in the states of the Pacific Region. Anchorage, Alaska, (left photo) is cold most of the year. Southern California (right photo) is warm all year round.

The city of Anchorage, Alaska, was once just a place where ships stopped. They were there to unload materials needed to build the Alaska Railroad. Today, Anchorage is the largest city in Alaska.

Two of the most important West Coast ports are Portland, Oregon, and Seattle, Washington. Neither one of these ports is near the ocean. Portland is 100 miles up the Columbia River. Ships go there to pick up lumber and other products. Seattle is 125 miles from the ocean. It is not on a river but on a large bay called Puget Sound.

Los Angeles, California, is the largest city in the Pacific Region. It is known for its busy highways, its beautiful beaches, and Hollywood, the movie capital of the world.

▶ **What are the names of three important ports in the Pacific Region? Write your answer here.**

_____

_____

Name _____   Date _____

Working in the Pacific Region

Look around your classroom. How many things do you see that are made of wood? Don't forget that paper is made from wood, too. The forests of Oregon and Washington provide many of the wood products we use.

The major product of Alaska is oil. The oil field in Alaska is bigger than any other in North America. A big pipeline carries the oil 800 miles from the northern part of Alaska to a harbor in southern Alaska. The pipeline is a very good way of transporting oil because roads cannot be built in the tundra areas of northern Alaska.

▶ **What do you think happens to the oil when it reaches the harbor? Write your answer here.**

_____

_____

After trees are cut down, the logs are taken to lumber mills where they are cut into boards.

More than half of all the fruits and vegetables you eat are grown in the West Coast states. California and Washington are also important centers for technology. Many large computer and software businesses are located in these two states.

Since all the states of the Pacific Region are near the Pacific Ocean, you have probably guessed that fishing is important. Service jobs are also very important. Many people in the region have jobs related to the tourism business. The Pacific Region is an area of great beauty. Each year, millions of people from all over the world visit the mountains, volcanoes, lakes, rivers, and exciting cities of the region.

➤ **How is the Pacific Ocean a resource for the region?**

_____

The giant redwood trees are a popular tourist attraction in California.

Name _____   Date _____

Chapter Checkup

➤ Darken the circle by the answer that best completes each sentence.

1. In the middle 1800s, people rushed to California to find
   - Ⓐ trees.
   - Ⓑ houses.
   - Ⓒ gold.
   - Ⓓ fruit.

2. The farthest edge of a country where few settlers live is the
   - Ⓐ West Coast.
   - Ⓑ frontier.
   - Ⓒ Pacific region.
   - Ⓓ tundra.

3. Chinese immigrants helped build a
   - Ⓐ gold mine.
   - Ⓑ wagon trail.
   - Ⓒ pipeline for oil.
   - Ⓓ coast-to-coast railroad.

4. The largest city in Hawaii is
   - Ⓐ San Francisco.
   - Ⓑ Honolulu.
   - Ⓒ Hawaii City.
   - Ⓓ Anchorage.

5. Many of the Pacific Region's biggest cities are
   - Ⓐ important ports.
   - Ⓑ in the Central Valley.
   - Ⓒ not near water.
   - Ⓓ in Hawaii.

6. The largest oil field in North America is in
   - Ⓐ Texas.
   - Ⓑ Puget Sound.
   - Ⓒ California.
   - Ⓓ Alaska.

THINKING AND WRITING

Imagine it is 100 years ago. You are traveling from the East to the Pacific Region. Which state would you choose to settle in? Why? Write your answer here.

_____
_____
_____
_____
_____

Unit 7 Skill Builder: Learning from a Diagram

What causes a volcano to erupt? Very deep down in the earth, there is melted rock called magma. During a volcanic eruption, the magma is pushed up through weaker rocks around it. When it reaches the surface of the earth, it is called lava. The diagram below shows you what a volcano would look like if it were cut in half.

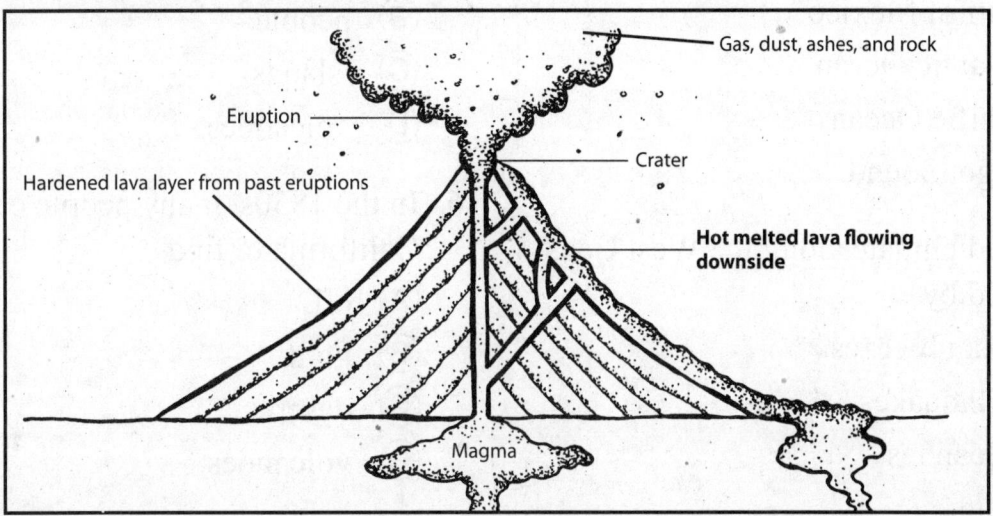

1. What is the bowl-shaped top of the volcano?

   _____

2. What are the sides of the volcano made of?

   _____

3. Trace one path of the magma to the surface.

4. Describe what you think it would be like to see a volcano erupt.

   _____

   _____

Name _____ Date _____

Unit 7 Test

▶ **Darken the circle by the answer that best completes each sentence.**

1. The West Coast states of the Pacific Region are next to the
   - Ⓐ Gulf of Mexico.
   - Ⓑ Atlantic Ocean.
   - Ⓒ Pacific Ocean.
   - Ⓓ Puget Sound.

2. The mild climate along the West Coast is caused by
   - Ⓐ ocean breezes.
   - Ⓑ earthquakes.
   - Ⓒ volcanoes.
   - Ⓓ faults.

3. During an earthquake,
   - Ⓐ there are strong winds.
   - Ⓑ there is heavy rain.
   - Ⓒ the ground shakes.
   - Ⓓ the climate is mild.

4. Farmers in parts of Alaska grow
   - Ⓐ oil.
   - Ⓑ tundra.
   - Ⓒ oats and barley.
   - Ⓓ fruits and vegetables.

5. Hawaii was formed by
   - Ⓐ earthquakes.
   - Ⓑ people.
   - Ⓒ islands.
   - Ⓓ volcanoes.

6. In the 1850s, many people came to California to find
   - Ⓐ oil.
   - Ⓑ gold.
   - Ⓒ deserts.
   - Ⓓ volcanoes.

7. Oil is the most important product of
   - Ⓐ Alaska.
   - Ⓑ California.
   - Ⓒ Hawaii.
   - Ⓓ the West Coast states.

8. The Pacific Region raises most of the country's
   - Ⓐ wheat.
   - Ⓑ cattle and sheep.
   - Ⓒ rice.
   - Ⓓ fruits and vegetables.

THINKING AND WRITING

How is the land of the Pacific Region different from the other regions you have studied?

_____

Name _____ Date _____

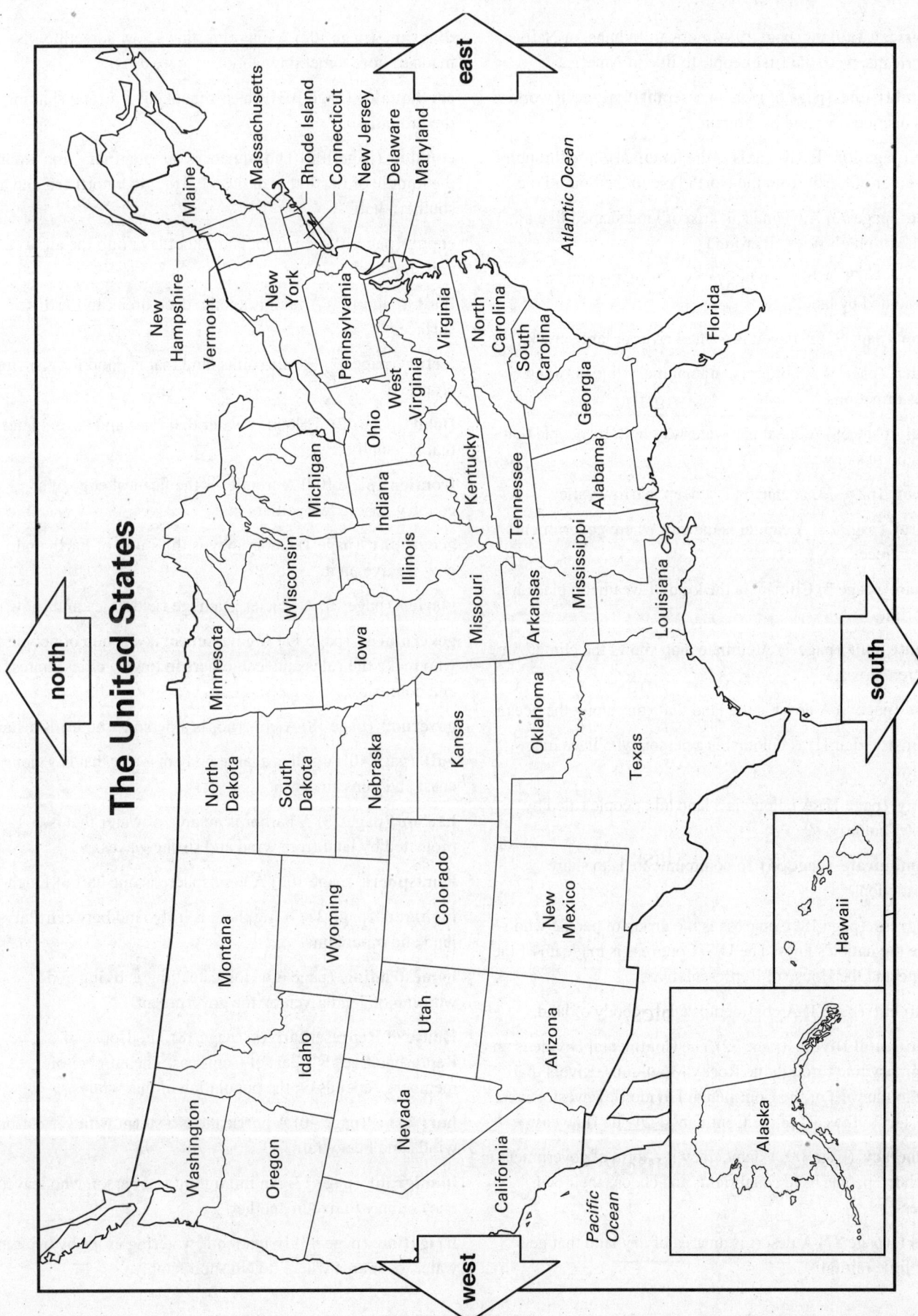

119

United States Map
Core Skills Social Studies, Grade 4

© Houghton Mifflin Harcourt Publishing Company

Glossary

American Indian (page 10) American Indians, or Native Americans, were the first people to live in America.

assembly line (page 65) On an assembly line, each worker does one job over and over again.

axis (page 106) Earth's axis is the imaginary line through the center of Earth from the North Pole to the South Pole.

basin (page 73) A basin is an area of land shaped like a bowl, with high sides all around.

bay (page 28) A bay is a body of water that is almost surrounded by land.

bayou (page 93) A bayou is a small river or large creek.

border (page 1) A border is an imaginary line between states or nations.

canal (page 58) A canal is a waterway built by people that links bodies of water.

canyon (page 73) A canyon is a deep, narrow valley.

capital (page 26) A capital is the city where government leaders meet.

climate (page 7) Climate is the kind of weather a place has over time.

climate map (page 7) A climate map shows the climate in different areas.

coast (page 5) A coast is the land that runs along the ocean.

colonist (page 11) A colonist is a person who lives in a colony.

colony (page 11) A colony is a land and people ruled by another country.

communicate (page 35) To communicate is to share information.

Congress (page 18) Congress is the group of people who make the nation's laws. The U.S. Congress is made up of the Senate and the House of Representatives.

continent (page 1) A continent is a large body of land.

Continental Divide (page 72) The Continental Divide is an imaginary line through the Rocky Mountains. Rivers that start to the west of the Continental Divide flow west. Rivers that start to the east of the Continental Divide flow east.

democracy (page 18) A democracy is a form of government in which the people have equal rights and choose their own leaders.

desert (page 87) A desert is an area of dry land that gets very little rainfall.

diagram (page 102) A diagram shows how something is made or how something works.

earthquake (page 103) An earthquake is a strong shaking of the ground.

equator (page 106) The equator is an imaginary line around the middle of Earth that divides Earth into a northern and a southern half.

erupt (page 105) To erupt is to shoot lava into the air, as a volcano does.

fault (page 103) A fault is a long, deep break in Earth's surface.

fertile (page 42) Fertile soil is land that is good for growing crops.

flood (page 42) A flood is water that rises and covers land that is usually dry.

frontier (page 109) A frontier is the farthest edge of a country, where few settlers live.

geography (page 1) Geography is the study of Earth and how we live on it.

glacier (page 73) A glacier is a huge field of ice and snow.

government (page 17) A government is a group of people who make the rules and lead others in towns, cities, states, and countries.

governor (page 18) A governor is a person who leads a state.

gulf (page 40) A gulf is a large body of water that lies along a coast and joins an ocean.

harbor (page 28) A harbor is an area of water that is protected by land from wind and strong waves.

hemisphere (page 106) A hemisphere is one half of Earth.

highland (page 27) A highland is hilly land between flat land and mountains.

homesteading (page 60) Homesteading is living and working on land given by the government.

House of Representatives (page 18) The House of Representatives is a part of Congress. The number of members depends on the population of their states.

hurricane (page 40) A hurricane is a storm with very strong winds and heavy rain.

immigrant (page 13) An immigrant is a person who leaves one country to live in another.

irrigation (page 87) Irrigation is watering crops by bringing water to an area where it is in short supply.

landform (page 5) A landform is a shape of the land, such as a mountain or hill.

lava (page 105) Lava is hot, melted rock from inside a volcano.

law (page 17) A law is a rule made by a government.

line graph (page 78) A line graph uses lines to show how something changes over time.

local government (page 17) A local government is a group of people who make the laws and lead the people of a town or city.

manufacturing (page 35) Manufacturing is making goods.

mayor (page 18) A mayor is a person who leads a town or city.

miner (page 78) A miner is a person who digs for minerals in the earth.

mineral (page 20) A mineral is something made by nature that is found in the earth. Silver is a mineral.

moisture (page 7) Moisture is how wet the air is.

Mormons (page 79) The Mormons are a religious group who went to Utah to find land and a place to worship.

Native American (page 10) A Native American is an American Indian, a member of one of the groups of people who were first to live in America.

natural resource (page 20) A natural resource is something from nature that people need and use.

physical map (page 5) A physical map gives information about types and shapes of land such as mountains and plains.

pioneer (page 60) A pioneer is a person who goes to live in a new place.

plain (page 5) A plain is a low, flat area of land.

plantation (page 48) A plantation is a very large farm.

plateau (page 5) A plateau is a high, flat area of land.

population (page 62) Population is the number of people who live in a place.

port (page 28) A port is a place where ships can load and unload goods.

prairie (page 57) A prairie is a large area of land with grass but few trees.

President (page 18) The President is the person who leads the United States.

prime meridian (page 106) The prime meridian is an imaginary line that runs north and south and divides Earth into an eastern and a western half.

recycle (page 20) To recycle is to reuse resources in order to keep from running out of those resources.

refinery (page 97) A refinery is a place where oil is cleaned and separated into different products.

region (page 3) A region is an area that land is divided into for study.

research (page 97) Research means studying things to find out about them.

reservation (page 77) A reservation is land set aside by the government where American Indian groups were forced to live.

rodeo (page 79) A rodeo is a contest for cowboys and cowgirls.

route (page 56) A route is a way or plan of travel from one place to another.

Senate (page 18) The Senate is a part of Congress. There are two members from each state in the Senate.

service (page 17) A service is something that helps people.

service job (page 19) A service job is a job in which a person does something to help other people.

settler (page 76) A settler is a person who goes to live in a new part of a country.

slave (page 13) A slave is a person who is owned by another person.

sod (page 61) Sod is blocks of dirt with grass growing in it.

solar energy (page 97) Solar energy is the energy from the sun's heat.

state (page 1) A state is one of the 50 political units in the United States.

suburb (page 32) A suburb is a small town or city that is near a big city.

Sunbelt (page 46) The Sunbelt is part of the southern United States, where it is usually warm and sunny.

swamp (page 42) A swamp is an area of soft land that is always wet.

table (page 40) A table is a kind of chart that allows facts to be compared.

temperature (page 7) Temperature is how hot or cold the air is.

transportation (page 32) Transportation is how people or goods travel from one place to another.

tundra (page 104) A tundra is a cold, treeless area where the ground is almost always frozen.

united (page 1) United means together.

volcano (page 105) A volcano is an opening in the crust of the earth through which melting rock, dust, ash, and hot gases are thrown up.

vote (page 18) To vote is to make a choice.

weather (page 7) Weather is how hot or cold it is. Moisture is also part of weather.

Answer Key

NOTE: For answers not provided, check that students have given an appropriate response and/or followed the directions given.

Page 1
Students should write the letters *U.S.* next to the United States on the map on page 2. They should put a check mark on Mexico.

Page 2
north

Page 5
Students should identify the West as having more mountains. They should write an *X* in the coastal plain on the East Coast on the map on page 6, an *M* on the Appalachian Mountains, and a *P* on the plateau near the Arkansas River.

Page 6
Students should write an *M* on the Rocky Mountains.
Pacific Ocean

Page 7
temperature and moisture
Students should circle the Pacific coast on the map on page 8.
cool summers

Page 8
warm winters

Page 9
1. D 2. D 3. C 4. C 5. A 6. C
Answers will vary. Accept all reasonable answers.

Page 10
Asia

Page 11
1680: 150,000; 1740: 900,000

Page 12
American Indians helped the colonists by teaching them how to grow food.
American Indians and colonists had different ideas about the way the land should be used.

Page 13
Students should circle Germany.

Page 15
1. A 2. C 3. B 4. B 5. B 6. A
Answers will vary. Accept all reasonable answers.

Page 18
Students should circle President.

Page 19
Manufacturing or Retail Trade.

Page 21
Students should answer that we know we have to be careful about how we use natural resources so we will not run out of them.

Page 22
1. B 2. C 3. B 4. D 5. B 6. C
Answers will vary. Accept all reasonable answers.

Page 23
1. 1950–2002 2. Mexico 3. more than 500,000
4. Answers will vary. Accept all reasonable answers.

Page 24
1. A 2. C 3. D 4. C 5. B 6. C 7. A 8. D
Answers will vary. Accept all reasonable answers.

Page 25
Students should write an *N* on Maine and an *S* on Maryland.

Page 26
about 100 miles

Page 28
Students should write two of the following as their answers: Narragansett Bay, Delaware Bay, Chesapeake Bay, or Boston Bay.
Students should trace any two of these rivers: Kennebec, Connecticut, Hudson, Delaware, or Potomac.

Page 29
1. B 2. B 3. A 4. A 5. C 6. B
Answers will vary. Accept all reasonable answers.

Page 30
They wanted to practice their own religion.

Page 31
It was too cold and late in the season to plant crops, and many Pilgrims died.
The American Indians had lived there longer.

Page 32
400 miles

Page 33
Providence, Rhode Island; Dover, Delaware; Annapolis, Maryland.
Both groups of colonists left England to practice their religions.

Page 34
nine states
Firefighters put out fires and save people.

Page 36
1. B 2. D 3. B 4. C 5. A 6. D
Answers will vary. Accept all reasonable answers.

Page 37
1. about $1\frac{1}{2}$ miles 2. about $\frac{1}{2}$ km
3. about $2\frac{1}{4}$ miles 4. about $\frac{1}{2}$ mile

Page 38
1. C 2. B 3. C 4. D 5. A 6. C 7. B 8. C
Answers will vary. Accept all reasonable answers.

Page 39
Students should write an *N* on West Virginia and an *S* on Florida.

Page 40
Students should circle Virginia, North Carolina, South Carolina, Georgia, and Florida.
Hurricane Katrina in 2005 caused the most damage.

Page 41
Bike routes should begin at the top of Virginia and end with an *X* at the southern tip of Florida.
Bike riding would get harder because the plains would change to highlands and the highlands would change to mountains.

Page 42
Mississippi River

Page 43
1. A 2. D 3. C 4. B 5. C 6. D
Answers will vary. Accept all reasonable answers.

Page 44
Richmond, Virginia

Page 46
the Southeast

Page 47
the Atlantic Ocean

Page 48
It is easier to build a railroad on flat land.

Page 49
Students should write *SEW* on the sixth picture and *SHIP* on the ninth picture.

Page 50
Students should name three of these: cotton, peanuts, rice, oranges.

Page 51
1. D 2. B 3. A 4. C 5. A 6. B
Answers will vary. Accept all reasonable answers.

Page 52
1. Georgia 2. Mammoth Cave
3. Okefenokee Swamp 4. Walt Disney World

Page 53
1. hurricane 2. swamp 3. Arms 4. gulf
5. France 6. Mississippi 7. rice 8. plantations

Page 54
1. B 2. D 3. C 4. D 5. A 6. A 7. B 8. D
Answers will vary. Accept all reasonable answers.

Page 56
Chicago

Page 57
plains
Students should circle the words *Great Plains* and *Central Plains*.

Page 58
Students should answer Lake Superior, Lake Michigan, Lake Huron, and Lake Erie.
Students should trace a route from the southern tip of Lake Michigan, southwest along the dotted line to the Illinois River, down this river to the Mississippi.

Page 59
1. C 2. D 3. B 4. B 5. A 6. C
Answers will vary. Accept all reasonable answers.

Page 61
plains or Great Plains
People use machines today.

Page 62
the eastern part

Page 63
Lake Michigan

Page 64
Students should draw a shipping route through Lake Superior, into Lake Huron, and into Lake Michigan.

Page 66
plains

Page 67
1. B 2. D 3. A 4. A 5. C 6. D
Answers will vary. Accept all reasonable answers.

Page 68
1. Lake Ontario
2. Check students' routes.
3. Lake Superior and Lake Huron

Page 69
1. C 2. A 3. D 4. C 5. D 6. B 7. C 8. B
Answers will vary. Accept all reasonable answers.

Page 70
450 miles

Page 71
Nevada

Page 72
the Great Basin

Page 76
rushing water

Page 74
1. C 2. B 3. B 4. C 5. A 6. A
Answers will vary. Accept all reasonable answers.

Page 78
July and January

Page 79
Utah
New businesses create jobs, and people move to the places where there are jobs.

Page 80
Montana, Wyoming, and Colorado

Page 82
1. C 2. B 3. B 4. A 5. D 6. A
Answers will vary. Accept all reasonable answers.

Page 83
1. It got bigger. 2. 1950
3. 1,200,000 4. between 1970 and 1990
5. The line might start higher and go down instead of up.

Page 84
1. B 2. A 3. B 4. C 5. C 6. A 7. A 8. D
Answers will vary. Accept all reasonable answers.

Page 85
Students should draw a line from Phoenix, Arizona, east to Austin, Texas.

Page 86
plateaus, highlands, and mountains

Page 87
three

Page 88
1. C 2. D 3. B 4. A 5. C 6. B
Answers will vary. Accept all reasonable answers.

Page 90
15,000
sickness and buffalo hunters

Page 91
the Navajo and the Pueblo

Page 92
291 years

Page 93
oil

Page 98
1. B 2. D 3. D 4. B 5. D 6. C
Answers will vary. Accept all reasonable answers.

Page 99
1. federal and state highways
2. Federal Highway 70
3. Federal Highway 380 east
4. west on 380, south on 285 to 62/180

Page 100
1. C 2. B 3. A 4. A 5. D 6. A 7. D 8. C
Answers will vary. Accept all reasonable answers.

Page 102
dry air
Students should circle the words *RAIN FORESTS* on the map.

Page 103
An earthquake is a strong shaking of the ground.

Page 104
Students should circle Juneau.

Page 105
Both Alaska and Hawaii have lots of mountains.

Page 106
the equator and the prime meridian

Page 107
1. B 2. D 3. B 4. C 5. C 6. C
Answers will vary. Accept all reasonable answers.

Page 108
They were all looking for gold.

Page 109
Answers might include to find a better life, to explore a new area, and to live in a less crowded place.

Page 111
California

Page 113
Answers may include Honolulu, Hawaii; Anchorage, Alaska; Portland, Oregon; Seattle, Washington; and Los Angeles, California.

Page 115
People catch fish from the ocean. The ocean and its beaches attract tourists.

Page 116
1. C 2. B 3. D 4. B 5. A 6. D
Answers will vary. Accept all reasonable answers.

Page 117
1. crater
2. hardened lava from past eruptions
3. Check students' tracings.
4. Answers will vary.

Page 118
1. C 2. A 3. C 4. C 5. D 6. B 7. A 8. D